Abraham Ritter

Philadelphia and her merchants

As constituted fifty @ seventy years ago

Abraham Ritter

Philadelphia and her merchants
As constituted fifty @ seventy years ago

ISBN/EAN: 9783337149260

Printed in Europe, USA, Canada, Australia, Japan

Cover: Foto ©Andreas Hilbeck / pixelio.de

More available books at **www.hansebooks.com**

PHILADELPHIA

AND HER

MERCHANTS,

AS CONSTITUTED FIFTY @ SEVENTY YEARS AGO,

ILLUSTRATED BY DIAGRAMS OF THE RIVER FRONT,

AND

PORTRAITS OF SOME OF ITS PROMINENT OCCUPANTS,

TOGETHER WITH

SKETCHES OF CHARACTER,

AND

INCIDENTS AND ANECDOTES OF THE DAY.

BY

ABRAHAM RITTER,

AUTHOR OF "THE HISTORY OF THE MORAVIAN CHURCH IN PHILADELPHIA."

PHILADELPHIA:
PUBLISHED BY THE AUTHOR.
1860.

PREFACE.

JUSTICE to authorship, and intelligence to the patron, have always claims upon the writer for a declaration, or an *eclaircissement* of the intent and purpose of a literary offering; but more especially in a work of historical pretensions, where authority for its records, or reliable tradition for its current incidents and anecdotes, may justly be a subject for the bar of inquisition; but though fearless of interrogatories, and even careless of criticism, it is but meet to clear the way to the volume, and show cause for effort, purpose, and effect.

The downhill of life is not always the decline of spirit. Old folks are apt to mount the throne of retrospect, and rejuvenate and play their early games over and over again; and not unlike Goldsmith's broken soldier,—

"Shoulder the crutch, and show how fields were won."

The past to us is as the present, and even more *picturesque*. It is like the sugar at the bottom of the cup, and needs but the stir of the lever of reference to sweeten the beverage of reflection; whilst the reflection

(3)

itself, is a tinge to the yellow leaf of the Oak of Time, renewing the verdure of the sapling of its infancy.

Hence, then, a retrospect of Philadelphia and her Merchants, as they moved the waters and enlivened the land some seventy years ago, rise before me, redolent of the fragrance of the blossom, the bloom, and the flower of the mercantile life of my early times.

But with all my claims to the prerogative of graphic imprint, acknowledgments are due to collateral testimony, artistic skill, and mind and matter beyond my own.

Firstly, then, my diagraphic display is from the quick conception and accurate delineation of my friend, Edwin F. Durang, Esq., a valuable, and very talented, and tasteful architect of our city, whose conception, from description of intent and purpose, is certainly unsurpassed; of whom it is but common justice to say, that he is as quick with the pencil as thought is to the mind, developing description as though the original were before him; all of which renders me, happily, safe in the drafts before you, especially as they have been tested by authority and linked by reliable tradition.

But mercantile *life* is set forth, and data, in dots and lines, is given, and whence the authority for that? To memory I appeal, and from it reveal the secrets from the recesses of sunken time.

Cradled in the very centre of my scope, growing and familiarizing with the life of my times, the things that were, charm the mental eye to the compass of the things that are. Memory lifts her pages, delivers her record with impressive force, and gives to the pen the eye of the mind.* Pardon me! I would not be egotistic—that would illy befit me—whilst memories combined, lateral and collateral, have given impetus to the work and identity to its portraiture.

There are antiquarians amongst us—venerable relics of the olden time—and happily so, for, but for such, even Moses and the prophets had slept unwept and unsung. Honor then to whom honor belongs.

Our venerable townsman, Mr. Charles Massey, is a veteran of time; and now, in his eighty-second year, is intelligent and elastic, with a well-regulated and well-stored mind, and a memory like a very chronicle. How could I be egotistic, after untrammeled intercourse with, and heavy drafts upon his tenacious memory.

Mr. Massey has evidently trained himself to observation, to plant results in his garden of reminiscence; whence also he has allowed me to cull the flowers of his mnemonic fancy, and perfume the page of accumulating history.

In process of this work, therefore, he has been a valuable adjunct, and his memory tested by comparison. Land-marks, and even history itself, emboldens me to present it as a reliable issue to the world and its bibliotheque. But enough! this old gentleman must appear in the vigor of his manhood, and the role of mercantile

---

* The Baron von Humboldt recently said, that History, or "Description," must be "written with the eyes."

life, in the body of this work, and there we may greet
him as an active spirit of his day.

When I began the work, however, I intended it
merely as an *Appendix* to another reminiscent gathering
of larger growth—a cursory review of local familiarities
of my youth; but matter grew and forced itself upon
me, even to the generation of a History; and being en-
couraged by older and abler heads than my own, ambition took the hint, spurred exertion, and inspired the
effort to do right whatever was worth doing at all.
Wherefore, whipping up my recollections, and propi-
tiating the good-will of my abettors, due diligence I
trust will show itself in the issue.

Notwithstanding all of this, " errors, omissions, and
exceptions" may possibly be charged upon your author;
but let the milk of human kindness mollify the criticism,
and the vail of forbearance darken the counsel that
cannot see the difficulties of perfection in all human
efforts.

CONTENTS.

(7)

CHAPTER VI.

CHAPTER VII.

CHAPTER VIII.

CHAPTER IX.

CHAPTER X.

CHAPTER XI.

CHAPTER XII.

CHAPTER XIII.

CHAPTER XIV.

CHAPTER XV.

CHAPTER XVI.

CHAPTER XVII.

CHAPTER XVIII.

CHAPTER XIX.

CHAPTER XX.

CHAPTER XXI.

CHAPTER XXII.

CHAPTER XXIII.

CHAPTER XXIV.

CHAPTER XXV.

CHAPTER XXVI.

CHAPTER XXVII.

CHAPTER XXVIII.

CHAPTER XXIX.

CONTENTS. 13

CHAPTER XXXIV.

CHAPTER XXXV.

APPENDIX.

ILLUSTRATIONS.

(15)

INTRODUCTION.

SEARCH and research appears to be the order of the day: by some, tributary to the arts and sciences; by others, to political, polemical, or professional interests; but by others to a more current and familiar attachment of a link remote in the bosom of Time—the former, however, more the forte of the hey-day of an author's prime; whilst the latter, touching the chain of recollections, is electrified by the spark from its source, and the flash of even a hundred years past comes vividly to his eye.

Our mortal is ever on the wane; but our immortal, jealous of its trust, awakes—as it were to the rescue—claims its throne, and spreads its rays over the fields of its existence. And thus lit up, the life of "the days when we were young" comes up in form, feature, and familiarity, greeting to the eye, and tangible to the very hand.

My object in this volume is not to call up the leaden clouds that hung over the pursuits of legitimate industry, nor even tinge them with a glimmer of the ills of unfortunates—for doubtless, three o'clock P. M., was as fatal to some then as it is now and has been ever since—but rather to show, who and what constituted the mercantile community, and the where of its active being.

I do not flatter myself into a phenomenon of literature, or

2 (17)

a competitor in historical issues, but I am happy to know that I have not passed Time's ordeal to nearly threescore and ten in vain. I *have* lived, seen, and observed; and assume to pen some of the results, in a review of Philadelphia and her Merchants of the olden time.

This self-imposed task is not without its *onus;* but neither is it without its pleasurable incentive. Memory will fondle with early scenes, and impels a *recueil;* association spurs it to life, and furtherance encourages the "search and research."

PHILADELPHIA AND HER MERCHANTS.

CHAPTER I.—INTRODUCTORY.

The Carrying Trade, and the principal operators in it.

THERE was a time, in the end of the last and beginning of the present century, when the "Carrying Trade" between the United States and the West India Islands, was a fruitful source of life to the commercial interests of Philadelphia. Her wharves were gay with streamers, from the smallest to the largest floating castles of the mighty deep, signaling their import, receiving the fruits of our own soil or presenting to our use and profit the riches of the soil of other climes.

Our intercourse with the West Indies was active, spirited, and rich in results; for whilst our Beef and Pork, Flour, Apples, Onions, Butter, Lard, and any other product of our fields or farms, were toothsome and desirable to the planter there, the issues of their soil, of Sugar, Coffee, Oranges, Lemons, Pine-Apples, etc., paid much better here, and laid the foundation of ease and comfort to very many of the retired dealers of that day.

The insurrection in St. Domingo, of 1792-3, however, created a hiatus for a time, in the untrammeled and profitable intercourse of our enterprise; but even that was propitious to the adventurer; and although intercourse was interdicted by

(19)

danger of traffic, and and embargoed by the savage hatred
of the blacks against the whites, there were some here who
dared the gauntlet for the prize of their temerity.

Abraham Piesch, of Swiss origin, a prominent shipping-
merchant of the day—a man of enterprise and risks—thought
it well to float a barge, invitingly laden, to the troubled
waters of St. Domingo, and his schooner "Fly" was forthwith
in command for the enterprise.

Her arrival on that coast was in common with—here and
there—a white speck, beating to and fro, apparently upon the
same errand, but to whom the fear of toil and danger was a
caution, and repulsive to their schemes, for they fainted in
courage, and faded in distance to fall into the arms of better
security, or drop their anchors in their own roadstead. Be
this as it may, our "Fly," true to her name, scented by the rich
odor of the garden before her, hovered cozily on its borders
until time and chance should offer their services.

The massacre had been desperate and unsparing; a single
white man only was reserved for their business purposes, and
him they marred and mutilated in his fingers and toes, and
nose too, to prevent his escape and secure his services to
whatever commercial interest might turn up. He was a
custom-house officer and important to their use.

Whilst the "Fly" was cruising about, and her officers spy-
ing out the land and the harbor for a rescue from their
anxious toil, or some medium of communication with the
shore, Thomas Thuit, the decrepit survivor of his race
there, was seen on his pony, pacing the sands of the shore as
eagerly peering for supplies to their exhausted market.

The "Fly" crept cautiously to his margin; hailing distance
bounded his nasal tones; the call was encouraging, and
won upon the hard salted Captain Wallace and his timid,

youthful supercargo, and the yawl was manned for a parley. Assurances of safety of persons and property brought the vessel to a proper mooring, and the very desirable cargo of apples, onions, lard, and various other edibles and culinary requirements, to an available landing.

To sell, was but a magical moment; and to buy, but the question of time to load.

Impromptu, coffee at five cents per pound was poured like sand into the hold of the craft, until the water washed her gunwales, and compelled her crew to creep over and wade through the bean to their bunks. She was loaded in bulk. Her return was joyous to her enterprising owner, and vastly cheering to the competitors in the West India trade.

This story I give as the party in interest and activity gave it often in my hearing, fifty years ago, to wit: the super-cargo, Jacob Ritter, Jr.

Rich as was the West India trade, we had even more to boast of. Europe, Asia, China, and Africa were represented at our margin by their merchandise. The towering masts of the dignified merchantmen betold their presence; and the "Yo, heave ho!" of the merry mariner heralded the delivery of their treasures.

The "Voltaire," the "Rousseau," the "Helvetius," the "Montesquieu," or the "Good Friend," in turn called the attention of our indefatigable Girard; and the independent wag of his head, and corresponding obedience of his queue, were duly present at the contributions to his wealth. Hemp, spun or unspun, raw or wrought and bar-iron, were commodities to sharpen, if possible, the already bright eye of their owner, to investigation, calculation and profit.

But he had other ways and means to fortune. Amongst

other shavings of nature, he discounted the dawn, and eclipsed it with Solomon's suggestion, "early to rise."

There were neither "steamboats" nor "telegraphs" to hasten news of arrivals below; the West India craft came up often by night, silently and softly, and the plash of their anchor died away on the circle of its making.

Girard, true to the proverb, taking daylight at its dawn, would slip from his gate to the wharf's edge, and sweep the Delaware with the besom of his powerful eye. An arrival at hand, or afar off, telegraphed itself to his vision, and fired his impulse to board the object of his search; and forthwith a "wherry," or a "batteau," laid alongside; and whilst his neighbors were dreaming of bargain and sale, he was making himself master of the market by his *coup de main.*

Our Henry Pratt, Pratt & Kinesing, Willings & Francis, Smith & Ridgway, James Vanuxem, Gurney & Smith, Jacob Gerard Koch, Summer & Brown, Louis Crousillat, Eyre & Massey, Piesch, Blight, Montgomery, Sims, and other mercantile wharf life, were all, in due course, at their respective posts, with their capacious ships breasting the docks or lining the outer edge of the wharf.

And this active life was enlivened by the music of the jolly tar, or the swarthy operator at the derrick.

Jack seemed to take the rattlings by surprise, and in a trice was in the cradle at the yard-arm, to bend or unbend the weighty canvas as duty required, and drop the significant "Aye, aye, sir," to the commanding officer below; whilst the negro song at the capstan or the derrick, echoed from wharf to wharf, until the south answered to the north, and the north continued to blend a cheerful response.

But there was even more cheering music than this to the eager ear of the expecting merchant.

The booming of a "big gun," five miles below, was the sure announcement of the safe arrival of an "East Indiaman," to which the non-interested, as well as the parties in interest, gave prompt heed. And men and boys, from all quarters, flew to the wharf to see the smoke and the flash as the "big ship" turned the point, and inquire "What ship is that?"

A gladsome sound from yonder Jersey shore,
    Repeats the cheer of India's guest below;
The echo rings! and men, just boys before,
    Fly to the wharf to glimpse the flashing bow.

Oh! glorious times of innocence and mirth,
    Unsmok'd, unsteam'd, the good ship seeks her berth;
In dignity she sweeps the silv'ry stream,
    Erst Neptune's toy, but now the merchant's theme!*

---

* New York was not our rival in those days. The "Park" was the boundary on the north, and the "Battery" was her lion on the south. Pearl street and Wall street were her emporiums of trade, whilst "Broadway" was the untrammeled highway for funeral pageant and military parade; and its sidewalk the inviting course to the several churches that then gave tone and character to its skirts. But her harbor, north and east, was the nest of small craft, better known by the stems that streaked the horizon than by the hulls that bore them.

In the fall of 1815, I saw the city and the port as above set forth. I saw a funeral procession pass up the middle of "Broadway," from below the "Park," unlet of wagon, cart, or dray, or any thing whatever beyond an occasional gig or pleasure wagon.

New York did not begin to develope till about the year 1816, when several of our principal silk houses and others went there on account of her open harbor during the winter, affording free ingress and egress to her commercial requirements.

Amongst the first of our emigrants, was the silk and ribbon house of Dru giere & Tessiere, from Market above Sixth street.

CHAPTER II.

The Hill of Callowhill Street, and a view of the Wharves from Callowhill to Arch street.

In reviewing the wharves from this point, I must first show up the hill and its appendages that led to the level below, not because there was any thing great there, but rather because dust and ashes have been increased by the incumbrance of that soil.

There was, on the north side of the hill, a *nest* or range of dirty-yellow frames, continuous from near Water street to the wharf, variously occupied by groggeries, boarding and lodging places, provision dealers, etc., where also hucksters congregated at night to raffle off their unsold poultry. The structure was antique and doubtless original, a very firstling of the Northern Liberties.

The wharves from this point were not as regular, free, and open as those below. Many of them, were enclosed and could not be passed without passing up one alley and down another; but they were no less important.

Britton's wharf took up a large space from the corner, southward, and was characterized as a ship-building point.

Taylor's dock was useful to the bath and revival of the jaded horse, as well as a pool for the boys to lave their fevered skin.

West's wharf was the recipient of countless loads of salt.

CALLOWHILL ST.

WHARF

TAVERN	BRITTON'S WHARF
DWELLING	THE SHIP
	NORTHERN LIBERTIES
DWELLING	BUILT ON THIS WHARF
	ABOUT 1799
DWELLING	

ST.

ALLEY

WOOD WHARF

STEWART & KNIGHT'S

BOARD YARD

1796

TAYLOR'S

DOCK

Wᴹ BROWN'S
BAKERY
1792

WOOD
WHARF

ALLEY

WEST'S
STORE

DOCK

ALLEY

SALT STORES

WEST'S WHARF
1791

ALLEY

WEST & JEANES

Wᴹ WEST
1791

SERVOSS &
SHOEMAKER
FLOUR STORES
1794

RIVER

WATER

VINE ST.

Wᴹ ___ WHARF

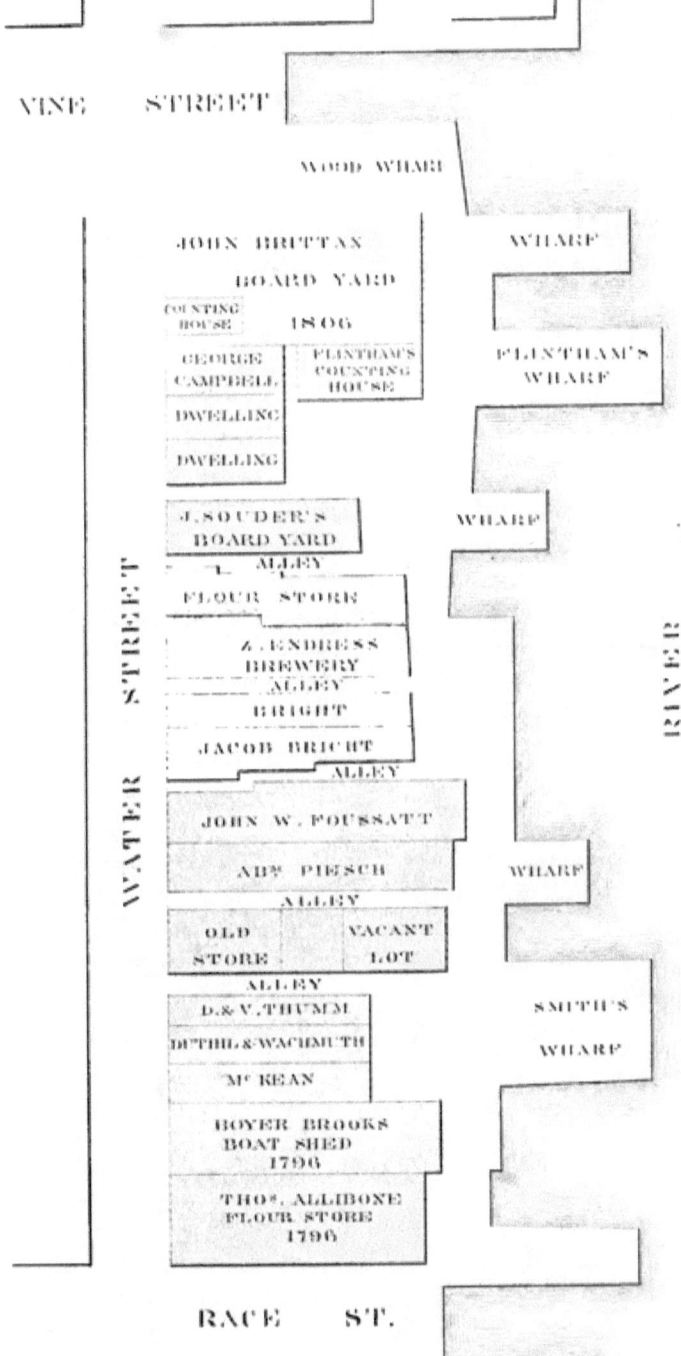

VINE STREET

WOOD WHARF

JOHN BRITTAN

BOARD YARD

COUNTING
HOUSE   1806

WHARF

GEORGE
CAMPBELL

FLINTHAM'S
COUNTING
HOUSE

FLINTHAM'S
WHARF

DWELLING

DWELLING

J. SOUDER'S
BOARD YARD

ALLEY

WHARF

FLOUR STORE

Z. ENDRESS
BREWERY
ALLEY

BRIGHT

JACOB BRIGHT

ALLEY

JOHN W. FOUSSATT

AB? PIESCH

WHARF

ALLEY

OLD
STORE

VACANT
LOT

ALLEY

D. & V. THUMM

DUTHIL & WACHSMUTH

McKEAN

SMITH'S

WHARF

BOYER BROOKS
BOAT SHED
1796

THO? ALLIBONE
FLOUR STORE
1796

RACE ST.

WATER STREET

RIVER

whilst Servoss and Shoemaker told off their income by numberless barrels of flour.

Wood and lumber, however, occupied an occasional intermediate wharf, and made up the measure of this line, more particularly defined in the annexed diagram.

The upper side of Vine-street wharf was graced with a very dirty dock, an original "bite" or harbor for wood shallops and other small craft, to load or unload, north or south; but it served also as another watering convenience for horses, being open to the street for their descent. But it was a muddy limb of the river, and, except at high tide, more to be avoided than desired.

Its adjunct was a wood wharf, and being a "good way up town," wood was supposed to be cheaper on Vine-street wharf than anywhere below; and the "Corder" was the recorder of profit by the result.

Lumber was landed at the south corner of Vine-street wharf, in the rear of John Britton's board-yard; and Eyre & Massey loaded their ship "Portia" here with lumber for Madeira, 1806.

After John Souder, at 141, William Flintham succeeded him in the premises as well as an oak-cooper as an extensive dealer in flaxseed, of which he shipped large quantities to Ireland, 1807.

Mr. Flintham was a very active and intelligent man, whose mechanical trade could not confine his genius; and passing from the cooper-shop to the counting-house, entered more extensively in the shipping business, but alas, in fine, not to profit.

A little below this the more active mercantile line began, and Bright, Piesch, Smith, Thunns, Dutihl & Wacksmuth, and others, were prominently located adjacent to their shipping interests on the wharf, or in the stream immediately before them.

Mercantile life was still more rife in the wharf line from RACE TO ARCH streets.

A ship-chandlery is always important to shipping interests, and Harvey & Davis, at the corner, were beneficiaries of this fact; but Henry Pratt, Pratt & Kintzing, Hodge, Summerl & Brown, down to Smith's alley, were very much of the active business life of this limit. There was, however, an ancient appendage to the convenience of this part in a block of frames of red hue, called therefore the "Red Stores." They stood in the middle of a pier, having a passage around them, and were used by Summerl & Brown, for storage, or any other convenience to their shipping requirements.* A full share of the wealth of the Indies, east and west, very often made a beautiful show on these wharves, of which, more particularly, our venerable contemporary, William Smith, was a bounteous recipient.

Mr. Smith was, or had been, a West India planter, though an Englishman by birth, but an owner of large domains in the West Indies, from which his income was very abundant. On his arrival in this country, he landed eighty thousand dollars in silver, (Spanish dollars), from which he derived his *soubriquet* of *Silver Heels*—but he was as often called "Gold-

---

* The Yellow Fever of 1793, first made its appearance here. The first victims were, 1st, Mrs. Maria Lemaigre, (widow of Peter Lemaigre, merchant, of 77 North Water street, 1793) a French lady; 2d, the stevedore of the ship that brought it to that wharf; and 3d, Mr. Wm. Burkhard, of 57 North Water street.

In after time, these "Red Stores" were the daily haunt of our former townsman, the father of our present Isaac Elliot, of Walnut street, conveyancer, who was the first Inspector of Bark of this port, under the appointment of Governor McKean.

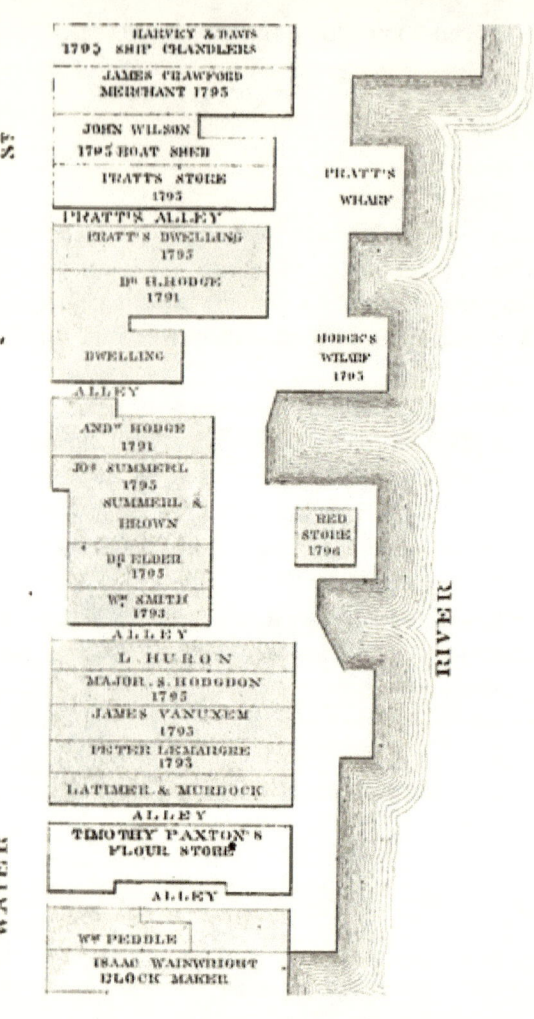

smith," to which his tall slim figure, dressed in black, with
knee-breeches, silk stockings and shining shoes, mounted with
good sized silver buckles, seemed to entitle him. His dignified ascent of Arch Street Hill, and his general appearance,
belongs to the history of his times.

In this immediate vicinity, our still existent, Francis
Jacoby, has claims to notice as a shipping merchant of the
day, having in 1807 and onward, been an active and extensive item of the commercial list.

James Vanuxem was not amongst the least of mercantile
prowess in this quarter; nor is the continuous business life of
Timothy Paxson, a well and widely known dealer in flour
to be passed in silence.* Nor yet Wm. Peddle's yard to his
cooper-shop, as a spot of busy scenes in these times of mercantile prosperity. His domain and Isaac Wainwright's
dock, and block and pump-maker shop, shut off the mercantile continuance here. And whilst Peddle often held this
wharf to his own use, though a great big ship did lay before
it, Wainwright divided the course to the ferry below by his
inlet for logs, which, whilst it served him to soak his timbers,
it very often soaked *ours*, as the treacherous logs rolled or slid
us into the dock as we tried our skill in running over them
from wharf to wharf.

"Come away to Billy Cooper's!" was the ring of the boat-
man's song, as he passed leisurely from the porch of Isaac
Smallwood's ferry house, at the corner, to his "wherry" at
the slip below; whilst the "horse boat"† rolled heavily under

---

* The prominent and equally respectable house of Latimer & Murdock,
flour merchants.

† As before observed, "steamboats" were not in being in those days. The
"horse boat" was a capacious affair—was drawn up to a convenient bearing

the plunge of the goaded beast thus urged to his passage to
the Jersey shore, the amiable publican the meanwhile taking
cognizance of the whole.

of the slip.   Horses, cows and cattle, generally, were led to its edge and urged
to the footing below.   Often a very difficult and dangerous operation

The oarsmen rowed at the bow and the stern of the boat.

There were no fancy offerings for aquatic excursions—no roar of escaping
steam, nor darkened horizon from the black volcanic eruptive of a Vesuvius
below. Such ideas had not yet burst from the bosom of their conception!
nor entered into the heart of man.

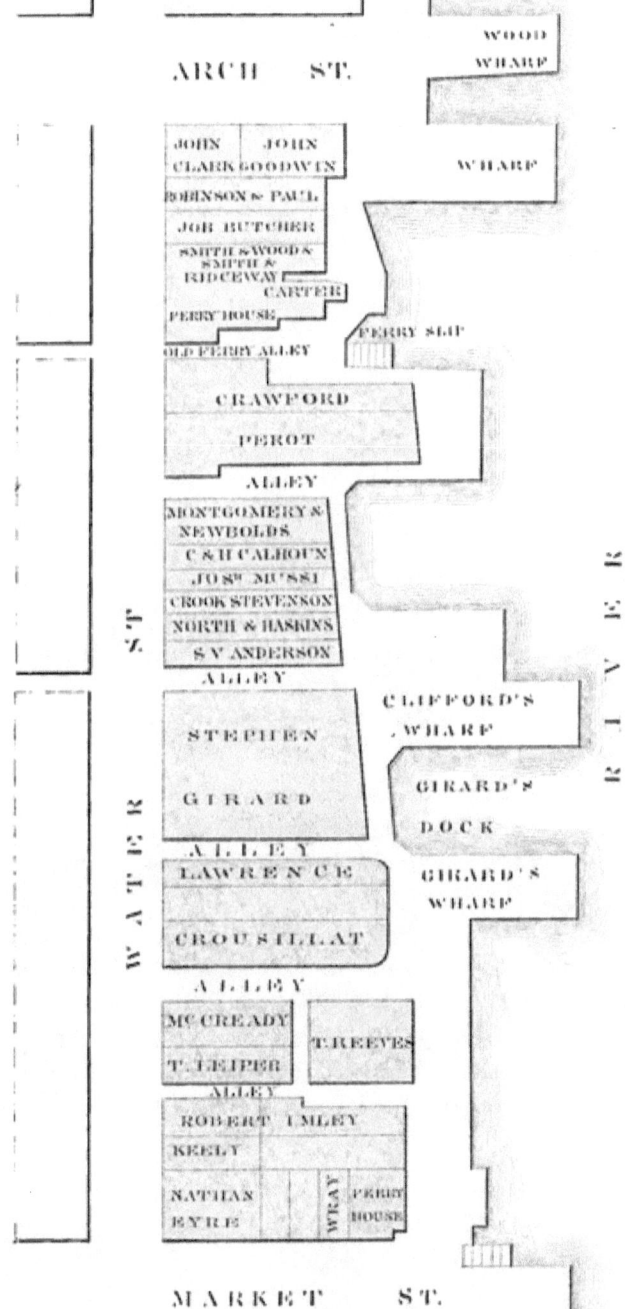

CHAPTER III.

The Wharves and their Tenants, from Arch to Market—Sharon Carter and his Cooper-shop—The Old Ferry.

Good, old-fashioned shallops hailed a berth at the foot of Arch-street wharf, passing to domestic comfort and economy, hickory, oak, pine, maple and gum, as fuel for the family hearth, at the hands of the Corder, as master of this wood-wharf.

The southwest corner store was a two-story rough stone building, weather-beaten and dark with age even in 1805. It was occupied by John Goodwin, ship-chandler, the father of our present cotemporary, Thomas D. Goodwin. Mr. Goodwin's tar-barrels abounded at his northern wall, one or two of which generally were filched to feed the flaming hilarity of an election night.

The wharf, here and at the rear of Smith & Wood, Job Butcher, and Robeson & Paul, extended a considerable distance outward, and formed the square of a dock immediately adjoining.

Granny Muff, a vendor of candies, etc., took a passage under this wharf, it being hollow underneath, and came out in the dock on the south side, whence she was gathered up, and landed in *full life.* She had accidentally fallen in on the north side. She certainly was not born to be drowned, for she lived to a good old age, and died a natural death.

This dock was an inlet to the flour store of Hugh & Joseph Ely, and Smith & Wood, and was covered at the head by a plank wharf or landing, for the convenience of their storage, as well as a passage to the Old Ferry, interrupted, however, by the small, brick cooper-shop of Sharon Carter,* where, and on the platform at the door, he and his boy Job,† rung the "Cooper's March," as a change to the "Yo, heave ho!" of the merry darky, as he showed up barrel after barrel from the hold of his sloop in the dock.

This plankway was of about eighty feet in width, and perhaps twenty feet in depth, including the platform of the cooper-shop.

The Old Ferry was a dilapidated affair already, in 1800; in use, perhaps, as a relief to the Arch-street throng, at the time the most popular.

There was an alley here, called the "Old Ferry Alley,"‡ leading to Water street, the south side of which was flanked by the grocery store and building of Samuel Crawford, whose

---

* Sharon Carter is still living, an active octogenarian, green in age, active and intellectual, and an admirable specimen of old times.

His drab suit of flowing coat, capacious vest, expansive knee-breeches, and fair top-boots, all easy of ingress and egress, surmounted by a fresh and florid countenance, dressed in natural bounty of flowing auburn curls, mark him well even in the distance.

He is now a collector of debts—more popular with the creditor than the debtor—and who, perhaps from the perseverance of his "fair-tops," have impudently dubbed him "Boots." He is now in his 88th year, even yet in the vigor of life.

† Job Lewis.

‡ This Old Ferry, and every vestige of it, is now merged in the shade of Delaware avenue; and the tail end of Crawford's store has been squared to the line; whilst the Alley leading from Water street to the Ferry has been built upon, and is even now covered by the large, brick iron-store of Reeves, Buck & Company.

rear wall extended far on the wharf, intercepting and inconveniencing a straight course, leaving but a small passage along the northern border, of some eight or ten feet, to the open wharf at the end of the building and around to the wharf and dock on the south, to the rear of the store occupied by Elliston and John Perot, William Newbold, afterward Montgomery & Newbolds, Gustavus & Hugh Calhoun, etc., to and along another narrow passage, down to Clifford's wharf, and the premises of Stephen Girard, whose dock here again narrowed the passage to admit the full length of his "Goodie Friends," or some other of his merchantmen, as they in turn breasted the inner guard, or hugged the outer escutcheon of his dock.

His, as were most of the yards of the Water-street houses, enclosed by an ordinary board fence, but in due time a substantial brick wall displaced his boards, and its gate was his daily outlet to Clifford's wharf, the usual landing of his merchandise.

The northeast corner of Clifford's wharf had sunk to low-water mark, the breast having given way at its base; it was called the Broken wharf, which at high tide made an available and convenient basin for bathing, and learners to swim, of which boys, and some of large growth, availed themselves without fear or favor, except from the dark and heavy streak that lay on the shed of Montgomery & Newbolds, sunning himself, fancied by the younger boys to be "Black Beard," which he seemed to enjoy.

Girard bought the wharf, but did not mend it, because of the depth of the water there, and the consequent difficulty of driving piles. In 1833, however, after his death, our city Fathers undertook it, and completed it by driving piles around it, and afterward extending it to the Warden's wharf. line.

The passage onward to Market street was uninterrupted by hook or crook; but being, for the most part unpaved, mud and mire, in wet seasons, moistened the path more than was desirable. The wharf was a straight line, and shallow—a mere landing.

Croussilat's counting-house was refined by a pavement to its entrance.

Jacob Dunton's sail-loft, and William Bethel's ship-chandlery, were at the head of Bickley's wharf, which opened at No. 13, before the times of Thomas Reeves, Imley, etc.

There was a ferry-house at the corner—a two-story frame—and the usual slip for the accommodation of boats and passengers. This was purchased by Stephen Girard; and the ferry once kept by one Scattergood, together with its appurtenances, were transposed, by the city Fathers, into more profitable issues to the city treasury.

But I must turn the corner here, to notice the life of the hill in the busy quarters of William Wray, whose variety of dry goods were unusual accommodations to the patrons of the ferry, from this and the other side of the river. His thrift here spread his domains from midway in the block down to the corner, and made him the owner.

Mrs. Wray was the active spirit of the counter—a good saleswoman.

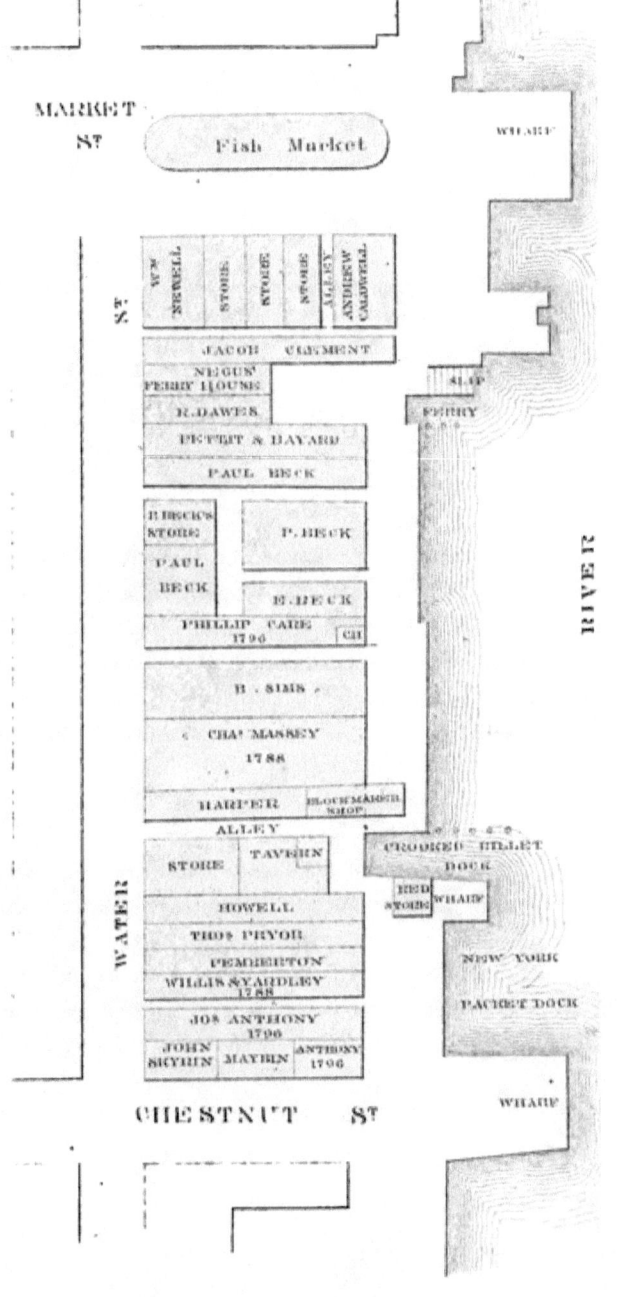

CHAPTER IV.

MARKET-STREET wharf was a wood wharf, and a fish market
also graced its entrance from the nether scope of the hill.

The hill here, as well as those of Arch and Race streets, was
quick and severe, but by grading and filling up, an easier
slope has been attained.

These hills were our winter's race course, a vent for the ebul-
lition of life and spirit. Sleds flew rapidly from the summit
to its base, at the expense of our heels and the profit of the
shoemaker, whilst our hearts did not return from *their* beat
until the wharf's level checked the impetus. Carts, drays and
wagons were few on these routes; there was little to mar the
sport, except now and then the slow, zig-zag course of a wood-
laden cart, as the poor beast, smarting under the lash, strove
to do his master's bidding.

The southwest corner of the avenue was a frame grocery
and fish store; and next but one below, was the ferry house
and slip of John Negus, in 1805.

The dock next below, was the harbor of the Wilmington
and Newcastle packets. Office on the wharf kept by James
Caldwell, in 1805, in charge of the "Fly," the "Morning Star,"
and the "Rising Sun."

A line of packet and schooners, fifty-five years ago, run to

3

New York by sea, from first wharf below the *Crooked Billet*, was established by D. & P. L'Homedieu, of New York. Two schooners, one the "David," and the other the "Philip," noted for their fleetness, constituted the line. Captain George Bird succeeded them, and kept up the line many years from the same wharf.

Wm. Warner's Wilmington packets, run from the first wharf above the *Crooked Billet*, opposite the blockmaker's shop: they were sloops.

In 1807, George Hand started an opposition in a larger class of boats, and heralded the "Diana," the "Telegraph," and the "Little George Eyre," at No. 8 below.

But there were fancy gatherings here more attractive than packets or pleasure boats. Peach boats took a hitch here, and drew hard upon the appetites and desires of men, women, and children.

Watermelons, in season, flew from hand to hand, with an occasional slip for the tooth and taste of the wistful urchin, who was not slow to decoy the throw from its proper rest. But sixpence would buy half a peck of good peaches, and small boys could be accommodated with a watermelon for a penny.

The most remarkable feature in this square was the famous "*Crooked Billet*," deriving its name from several crooked pieces of wood transversely arranged, and designating the tavern, at the head of the dock, kept by Edmund Byrne in 1799.

There was a deep cut into the wharf, intercepting the straight course of the wharf or passage, leaving a very narrow pass to and from the tavern above and the wharf proper below; while a blockmaker's shop at the corner of the narrow pass ever impeded or delayed the wayfarer as he would pass onward.

The passage, in itself, around this corner, up the north side of the dock to the alley, and again down the south side to tavern and the wharf proper, was a dangerous route even in daylight, but much more so at night; and the life of one of our valuable citizens, Mr. Isaac Jones, paid the penalty of an adventure here after nightfall, December 2d, 1807, in his sixty-fourth year.

It was a dingy, dismal spot, and a complete man-trap; for several others were drowned in their ignorance of the interruption of the line.

About midway of the wharf, on the south side of this deep cut, and nearly opposite the blockmaker's shop, on the very edge of the dock, there was another nest of red stores—frames, occupied as an iron store, by a certain Joseph Roberts.

The wharf in front of these stores was the mart for the exhibition and sale of ships' "cambooses," stores, etc., made, prepared or furnished by E. G. & W. Ashbridge, in 1799.

In this immediate vicinity, a little north of the dock, another very valuable member of the community, was cut off without one minute's warning.

On the night of the 24th, 25th of August, 1803, a fire occurred at the store of J. & P. Daniels',* between Water street and the wharf; and at early morn our neighbor, Mr. John Clark, whose store and dwelling was at the corner of Arch and Water streets, went forth to see the ruins; in passing which, a chimney fell and smote him to death. And in five

---

* Daniels's was an embryo shot factory, whence it is supposed that our successful in that business—Paul Beck, took his cue and built the tower to perfect the scheme.

minutes from the time he left home, he was returned a corpse.

This catastrophe spread a gloom over every domestic circle of the neighborhood of that morning, for Mr. Clark was highly respected and well beloved, being very popular for his many *virtues*.

Paul Beck, of whom more hereafter, was owner of several contiguous lots in this compass, variously planted with small tenements, and mostly in the tenancy of small dealers, provisions, ship-stores, sail lofts, etc.

For the tenancy of the wharves onward to Chestnut street, I must refer the reader to the diagram, as most of the incumbents opened on Water street, and must reappear in the detail of that line.

The wharf line from the Red Store wharf, was a straight line to Chestnut street; but the dock immediately north of Chestnut street, was the receptacle of the "Nantucket and New Bedford packets," bringing lamp oil of various qualities to the store of Willis and Yardley, at No. 21, the principal oil merchants of the day, 1802.

This firm afterward was extensively engaged in the flour trade, upon the same premises.

Joseph Smith occupied the corner as an iron store, whilst Smith & Carson occupied the second story as counting-house to their general commercial enterprise.

CHESTNUT ST

WATER ST

ST

DESMOND BYRNE | WATSON & PAUL

ALLEY

Wᵐ PRICHETT

SAMˡ MORRIS

JAMES STOKES

EYRE & MASSEY

Wᵐ SYKES | RED TAVERN

THOMAS LOYD

JOHN WELSH

SMITHS LOT

TUN ALLEY

ISAAC HAZLEHURST | J. WILCOCKS 1796 INDIA STORES IN 1789

1789

S. ALLEN

STORE

STORE | J. S. WALN'S ESTATE

STORE | JOHN GARDINER 1805

R. CORRY'S STORE

ALLEY

STONE STORE

NICKLIN & GRIFFITH

GRANT | BARBERS & ANNESLEY 1800 T. P. COPE 1812

WALNUT ST

RIVER

INDIA WHARF

CHAPTER V.

Wharves—Chestnut to Walnut—James Stokes—Eyre & Massey—Tun Alley—
India Wharf—Robert Morris.

A WOOD-WHARF here was again prominent for the accommodation of the citizens.

There was also a deep cut or dock on its southern border for the use and behoof of the Burlington packets, in 1805. At the head of this dock, at the southwest corner of Chestnut street, our late wealthy citizen, James Paul, in company with John Watson, under the firm of Watson & Paul, in 1802 and onward, was located in the provision trade, and that to a very successful issue.

The passage between their front and the wharf log was narrow, and led round and up a twelve-feet alley, on the south side of their store; and narrowing to a mere foot-way in front of Wm. and John Pritchards' store, next below, to the south line of which the dock extended to Chestnut street.

Here the wharf deepened to sixty-seven feet, including the fronts of Samuel Morris, James Stokes, and Eyre & Massey's stores and counting-house, No. 28* South Wharves.

From this onward, the wharf narrowed to Tun alley,† having a basin or dock in front of Sykes', Lloyd's, Welch's, and Smith's wharf and lot.

---

* And Massey & Shoemaker, in 1799.

† Tun alley derives its name from the tavern's sign at its foot, being three miniature tuns, crossing each other, and suspended over the door.

India Wharf adjoins here, a very important point of commercial interest.

It was the harbor for the "East Indiamen," and faced by the extensive stores of Robert Morris, of Revolutionary times, and occupied by him and Peter Whitesides, in 1789, and in 1795 by John Wilcox. Tone and Tenor attached to these domains even yet in the early part of this century.*

The "India Stores"† were largely capacious, and the wharf was quite equal to the call. It had a breast of one hundred and seventy feet. The line, however, was broken by a short pier near its southern limit, and forming a dock on each side; the whole, however, appurtenant to its own stores, with a share to the store of Jacob S. Waln.‡ A private alley and the plot

---

* This Mr. John Welsh was the sire of the present respectable mercantile house of S. & W. Welsh, of No. 60, South Wharves, and the root of *their* mercantile pursuit.

† These stores belonged to Robert Morris; but Thomas Willing, afterward President of the original United States Bank of 1791, John Swanwick, and others, were here in the East India trade.

Mr. Morris bought the United States frigate "Alliance," and fitted her up and out for the East Indies, in which she made but *one* voyage to China, and was condemned on her return as unseaworthy, dismantled, and drifted to Petty's Island—where 'tis said some of her ribs yet perpetuate the fact of her existence.

On her voyage to China, she had for her commander, Thomas Reed; first-mate, the late Commodore Dale; and for supercargo, the late George Harrison, of Chestnut street.

It is recorded thus: "September 19, 1788, the ship 'Alliance,' Thomas Reed commander, and George Harrison supercargo, arrived from Canton, consigned to Isaac Hazlehurst & Co.," of which Robert Morris was the company.

The ship was seven hundred and twenty-four tons register: a very large ship in those days.

‡ Jacob S. Waln occupied the south side of the India Stores fifty years ago. He afterward purchased the store south of it, where his son, S. Morris Waln, continues mercantile operations.

of the estate of John Gardner, to Thomas P. Cope's wharf, next below.

Cope's wharf was an unbroken line of one hundred and sixty feet, from India wharf to Walnut street.

Mr. Cope was a prominent and became an opulent shipping merchant in the Liverpool trade—the owner of several very large ships of most successful issues. 1793 to 1805 knew him as a dealer in dry goods, at No. 19 North Second street, at the corner of Pewter Platter, now Jones' Alley.

1812 lit him up as an extensive shipping merchant and shipowner at Walnut street wharf;* and 1854, closes his career as a millionaire, or something near it.

Mr. Cope was eminent for his liberality in benevolence, and furtherance of public improvements: a willing leader in all charitable requirements.

He died in November of that year in the eighty-seventh year of his age, a man of unblemished character, esteemed as well for his manners as his means.

* In 1802, Barking & Annesly were extensively engaged in the tobacco trade on these premises.

CHAPTER VI.

THERE was no break in the wharf-line from Cope's down to
Ross's wharf, but a straight line of one hundred and sixty-one
feet from the south side of Walnut street, affording a mere
passage way or side walk to the projection of Ross's wharf,
which was of some depth, and bordered a spacious dock of the
above width of one hundred and sixty-one feet, where ships,
brigs, or small craft, could and did lie snug and safe.

Below this, another dock to Morton's wharf, which was
fifty feet wide, thence a dock to Morris's wharf, and thence
another dock to Hamilton's wharf, also large and capacious;
leaving the passage, or shore, a mere way, except where a projection enlarged the border.

The face of this front showed up a brick store at the corner
kept by James Yard, a shipping merchant in the St. Croix,
Spanish Main, Havannah and European trade. Whilst next
below, a large coal yard of ninety-five feet front, was the
emporium of Liverpool coal—not Schuylkill County—used in
that day mostly by blacksmiths; and there was a blacksmith-
shop in the yard, doubtless ever ready to test the quality of
the *coals*, as was common to say in those days.

A pair of old brick stores adjoining this and a ten-feet alley,

WALNUT St

STORE STORE STORE	JAMES YARD
STORE	THOMAS'S
STORE	COAL-YARD.
DWELLING	BLACK-SMITH
DWELLING	SHOP
DWELLING	
DWELLING	STORE
DWELLING	STORE
ALLEY	STORE

DWELLING | H. RALSTON'S 1793 C. 1601-58 | McNAUGHT'S

48

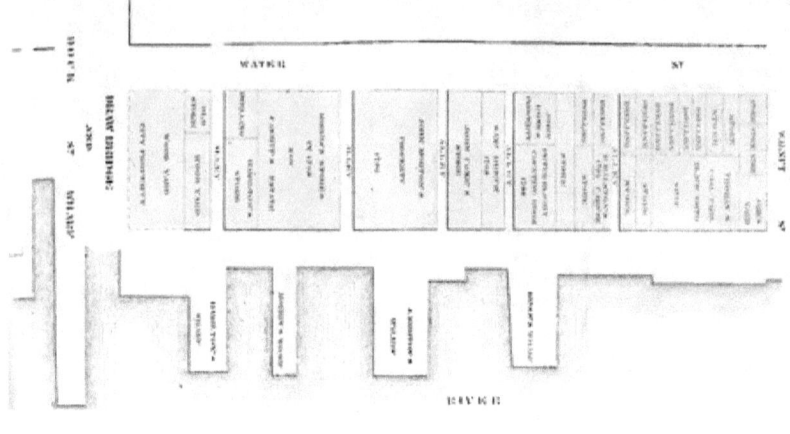

gave the lower corner for the counting-house of our late valuable and venerable fellow-citizen, Robert Ralston, of whom more hereafter. Mr. R. was here in 1793.

Peter Blight occupied the wharf front of John Ross's, Water-street stores. And our present venerable Samuel Breck, was located in his mercantile pursuit next below. These premises cover eighty-five feet of front, (1797.)

The well known firm of Savage & Dugan were at this point, after Peter Blight, extensively engaged in the West India and European trade. Counting-house on Ross's wharf.

John Cox's store, counting-house and wharf, takes up thirty feet next below, and an alley of twenty feet separates him from the premises of John Morton, which covered eighty-one feet front.

Morris's stores,* now belonging to the Fassit Estate, adjoined below, and covered seventy-seven feet of wharf front.

Hamilton's stores and extensive front of seventy-five feet, follows here, but divided by an alley to Water street. The wharf here adjoining was a commercial wharf, but for some years past has been a wood wharf.

The lot south of this to Dock street, was an open lot, belonging to the city, and the wharf in front an unindented line to the dock.

This dock was an inlet, answering for unloading of small craft, as well as for the laving of horses, of which we boys often availed ourselves of an extra hour for amusement, by swimming our neighbors' horses, which sometimes by a freak of their heels swam *us* to the amusement of lookers-on. But there was utility in the dock besides; horses were often rescued from

---

* This Morris was the root of the Brewer family of Morris's, afterward in Second street, between Arch and Race streets, now the premises of the late Robert Newlin.

drowning by being towed to this declivity, when by accident
they had fallen into the river, if any way near, or by res-
tiveness in a horse-boat, or backed over the wharf, their lives
were at stake.

The dock, the bridge, the scows and the mud that lay
under the bridge and in the dock, are fully before the public
by our Watson, and hence no more of that from me.   But on
the south side of Dock street there was an old store, flanked
on the south by a wide alley to Water street, and bounded by
other old stores; but the line of the wharf was unbroken from
the dock, southward, and the receptacles of wood to the glory
and profit of the corder.

There is, however, an item in my range here, omitted, or
forgotten, by our Watson, which, although foreign to my
special purpose, belongs to the early times of Philadelphia's
famous Dock street; and as such, I call it up here.

There was on the south side of Dock street, near Front
street, the old fish-house, a regular fish-market,* with belfry
and bell, whose tongue heralded far and wide the arrival of
fresh fish, besides announcing to the befogged watermen, in
their passage to and from the Jersey, of the whereabout of the
landing.

The old ferry below Arch street, was a competitor in the
trade and the accommodation; and fishmongers and fish-eaters
were called to order by the twang of the bell here also, and
the temptation to Epicurean fancy.

From this point to Spruce street, there is nothing particular

---

* In 1764, the Common Council of the City resolved to build a fish-market,
for the purpose of filling up the vacancy between the new stone bridge on
Front street, and the wooden bridge on Water street.   The stone bridge was
built in 1763.   The fish-market was still standing in 1830, altered into a
store.

to note, except the wharf estate of the Stamper family, on the south side of Dock street, and represented by the late Richard Willing, as guardian or trustee of the grand-children of Joseph Stamper; all of this sixty years ago and more.

John Waln, well known in his day as a vendor of corn, supplied the merchants with the article at all times from these premises.

CHAPTER VII.

Wharves and Stores—Spruce to South.

SPRUCE-STREET wharf was from time immemorial, as it is to this day, the oystermen's resort for supplies to their respective oyster cellars, shops, and subsequently more refined restaurants, seeing that the boatmen congregated here to vend the fruits of their tongs from the depth of Egg-Harbor, Cove, Chesapeake Bay, etc., where the active market expedited their return to the bivalve families beneath their floating interference with their snug repose below.

In 1796, and long after, Jesse and Robert Waln were prominent merchants at the corner of the wharf, and *theirs* was the first projection of any depth into the river, and broke the monotonous line of Spruce-street wharf: it was known as Waln's wharf. They were extensively engaged in the London and East India trade for many years.

Snowden & North, ship-chandlers, occupied the store adjoining, but were not proprietors of more wharf than the mere passage, hemmed by the wharf-log, to the premises and projection of Levi Hollingsworth & Son, upon which, on the northern and southern lines of their dock, was planted their stores for the reception and issue of flour, having an area of dock between the stores.

These gentlemen were very extensively engaged in the flour trade.

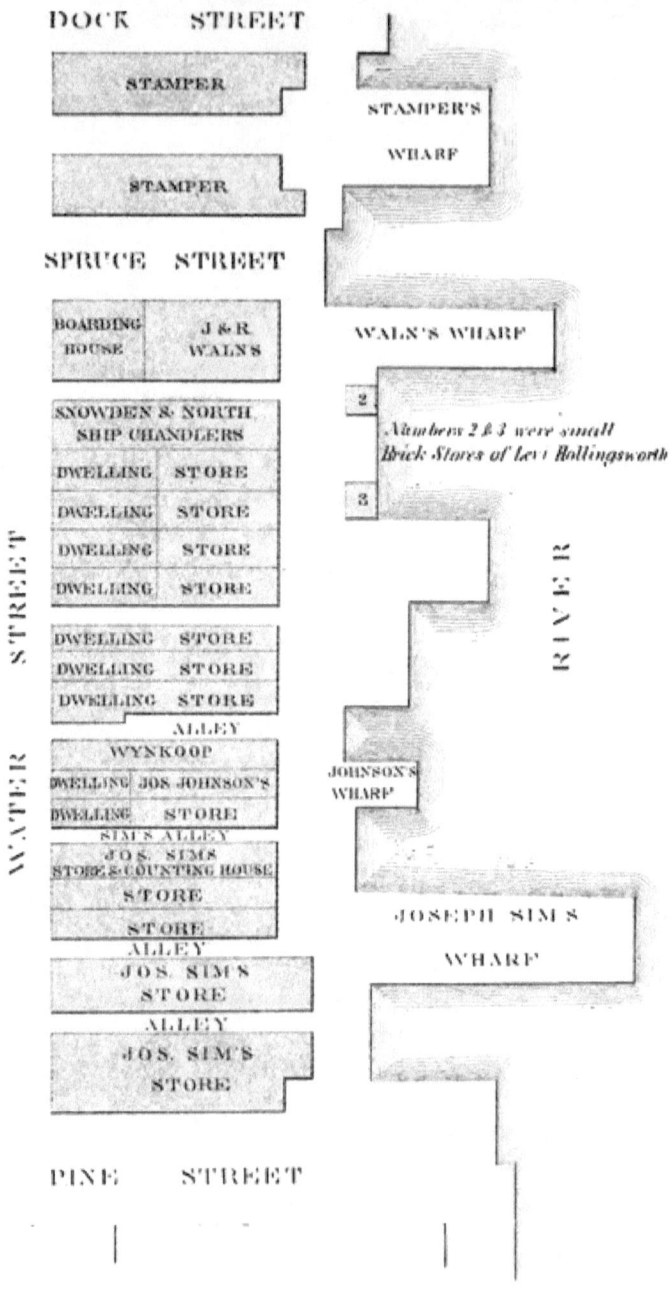

DOCK STREET

STAMPER

STAMPER

SPRUCE STREET

STAMPER'S

WHARF

BOARDING HOUSE	J & R. WALNS

WALN'S WHARF

2

SNOWDEN & NORTH SHIP CHANDLERS	
DWELLING	STORE
DWELLING	STORE
DWELLING	STORE
DWELLING	STORE

Numbers 2 & 3 were small Brick Stores of Levi Hollingsworth

3

DWELLING	STORE
DWELLING	STORE
DWELLING	STORE

RIVER

ALLEY

WYNKOOP

DWELLING	JOS JOHNSON'S
DWELLING	STORE

JOHNSON'S WHARF

SIM'S ALLEY

JOS. SIMS STORE & COUNTING HOUSE
STORE
STORE

ALLEY

JOSEPH SIMS

JOS. SIMS STORE

WHARF

ALLEY

JOS. SIM'S STORE

WATER STREET

PINE STREET

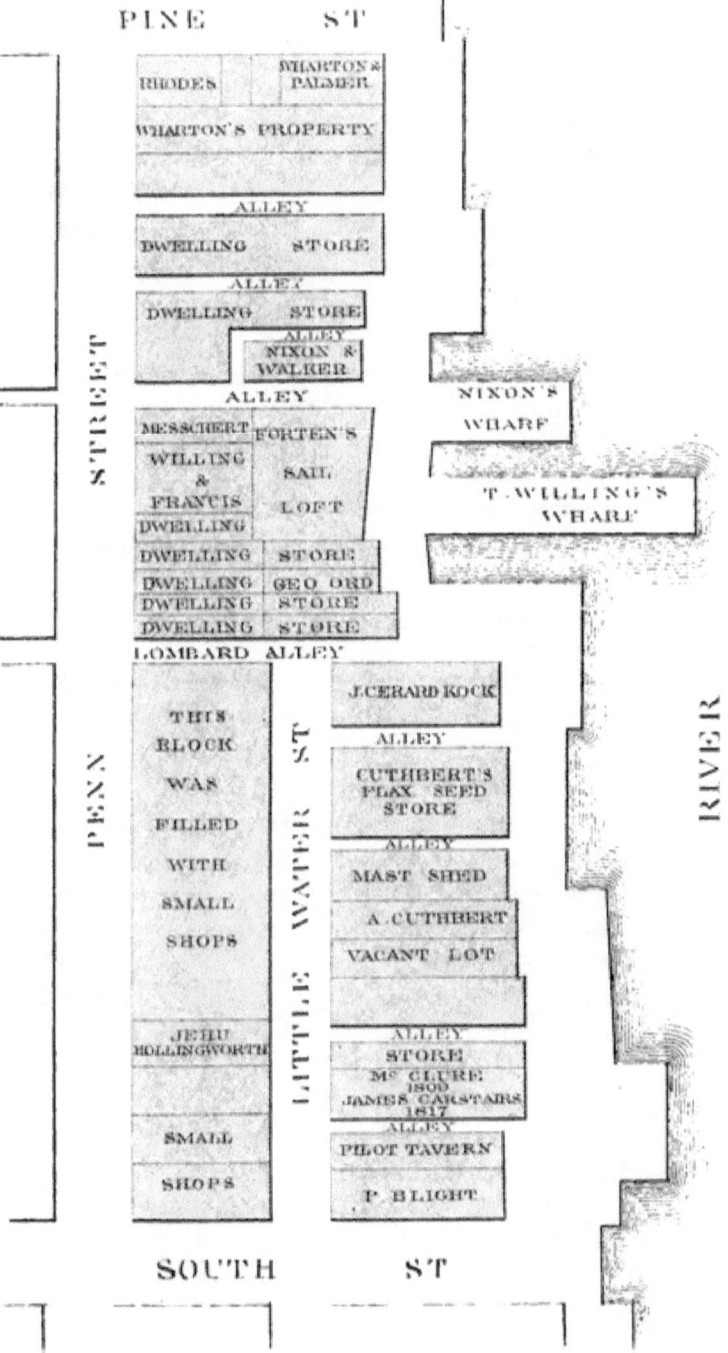

There was a fifteen-feet wide alley here adjoining Snowden & North's, to Water street; and the dock below, appurtenant to Hollingsworth's stores, was *formed* by an extension of Paul Beck's wharf, even deeper than the pier above.

Another dock here led to a jut or small pier, belonging to Joseph Johnson, whose ship-chandlery faced the wharf.

From the above fifteen-feet alley, seven stores occupied the upper edge of the wharf, down to Johnson's ship-chandlery, which was flanked by another fifteen-feet passage to Water street, and gives us the stores of the eminent merchant Joseph Sims, of whom also more hereafter.

Immediately in front of the alley, a small dock washed the extensive wharf of Mr. Sims, known as Sims' wharf, directly in front of his stores, where the several ships of this opulent and popular merchant of 1797, and onward, hugged the breast of their safeguard 'till orders came to "let go the hawser."

From this pier to Pine street, the inner wharf-line was straight and continuous, leaving an extensive dock in front of Sims's property, whilst a part of his stores extended above and below the pier.

Pine-street wharf was not extended, but was continued a straight line across the foot of the street to a pier or projection about one hundred feet from the corner, nearly opposite an alley from the wharf to Penn street.

The direct course here is, and apparently ever has been, obstructed by a row of stores on the south side of the hill from Penn street, extending considerably below the wharf line of the north side of the street, compelling passengers to turn to the left for the wharf, or to the right for Penn street.

The corner store of the wharf was occupied by Wharton & Palmer, as early as 1797, and onward to and beyond 1807.

This Mr. Wharton, was Mayor of the City in 1798, and

for many years after.   He was bold, intrepid, and very active,
ready at a moment's warning to quell a riot.   His appearance
at such gatherings with staff in hand, and hat tipped a little
on one side of his head, with firm step, and independent
authority, would scatter the ire and the fire of the most fero-
cious mob.   Philadelphia never had a more efficient and
popular municipal officer.

The wharf-line from Pine to South had several minor
indentations, but there were two of extra dimensions, to wit,
Nixon's wharf and Willings' wharf, adjoining their large
dock, embraced by this and the wharf above.

The stores of Thomas Willing and Willings & Francis,
were extensive, bounded by a twenty-feet alley to Water
street, on the north, Lombard alley on the south, and on the
west by Penn street.

James Forten, a colored man, occupied the upper part of
Willings' stores as a sail-loft, where he pursued the trade of
sail making in 1805, and for many years after, and until
industry and perseverance handed him over to retirement
and competency.

Mr. Forten was a gentleman by nature, easy in manner, and
affable in intercourse; popular as a man of trade or gentleman
of the pave, and well received by the gentry of lighter shade.
He was very genteel in appearance, good figure, prominent
features, and upon the whole rather handsome than otherwise.*

But James was ambitious, though certainly unassuming.
He had a family, and of course strove for a respectable platform for its members; and to this end it was said of him that

---

* He was brought up and learned the trade of sail-making, under charge
of Robert Bridges, of Frout below Lombard street.

he coveted to wed his daughter to a whiter species at some sacrifice of his fortune. This was an *on dit* of the day.

The several occupants of the line from Lombard alley to South street, being located on the diagram, spares me here, inasmuch as some of them must reappear on my return through Penn street.* I must however close up the square with the domain and identity of Peter Blight, who, though last in the survey, was not the least in the active business life of our Wharves some sixty years ago.

* It may be proper to note here, that Penn street and Little Water street, are two distinct avenues between the wharf and Front street.

Little Water street is about one hundred feet west of the wharf, and Penn street about seventy-five feet west of that.

Little Water street was a kind of back-front to the wharf-stores; and the position and course of Penn street, in many cases, gave it business connection with Little Water street.

Penn street runs from Pine to South street, but Little Water street takes the name of Swanson street, from South street to the Swede's Church and Navy Yard.

CHAPTER VIII.

Streets—Little Water and Penn streets—Jehu Hollingsworth—John Swan-
wick—Jacob Gerard Koch—Willings & Francis—M. H. Messchert—Samuel
Rhodes—Daniel Dolby—Sketch of Joseph Dolby, Sexton of Christ Church
—Nixon & Walker.

HAVING thus presented the Wharves, and their general
front, from Callowhill to South street, by diagram and description derived from documental and corresponding mne-
monical authority, as well as practical observation, I take
my course northward, from South to Pine streets, in search
of the principal mercantile life of that compass.

After passing some small tenements from the corner, the
counting-house and stores of Jehu Hollingsworth present
themselves. Mr. H. was a merchant of some account, being
largely engaged in the West India trade.

His counting-house was at No. 47 Penn street, but his
stores were continuous from Little Water street to the
wharf.

John Swanwick, a shipping merchant, held a prominent
position at No. 20 Penn street—for, in addition to his mercantile pursuits, and his general association with ships and
cargoes of sugar, teas, coffee, etc., he was a politician of
1796-97-98, a Democrat of some importance, and as such
was elected, and sent to Congress about 1795-96, where he
was also an opponent of Jay's treaty; these extraneous mat-

ters being adverse to merchandising, drew heavily upon his prosperity, which, perhaps with other evils, suppressed a successful issue to his labors.

Our old friend, Jacob Gerard Koch, and neighbor of Ninth and Market streets in 1806-7, was a prominent merchant of the day, 1796, and after, at the south corner of Lombard alley and Little Water street to the wharf.

Mr. Koch was a Hollander, an importer and vendor of German linens—articles at that day and long after, until about 1816, of easy sale and interesting profits, which told very sensibly in the treasury of this operator.

It is related of him, that in a crisis of his times, he was supposed to be ruinously damaged; but at a festive party—of which he was a guest—where, perhaps, sympathy shaded the scene, he lit up the countenances of his companions by an exhibit of available securities of $700,000, saying, "I'm not ruined yet!"

Mr. K. was a very large, corpulent, and heavy man, whom three hundred weight would scarcely excuse. He was of very cheerful and happy temperament, promoted, no doubt, by as liberal a disposition; which, with his punctuality and probity in all his business transactions, responded to each other, and built up his moral, personal, and financial weal.

He was withal as patriotic as he was liberal; and besides lending himself to the Western expedition, offered his purse in after time to palsy the prowess of England on the high seas.

In the war of 1812, a subscription was opened by private patriotism to build a frigate for the public service; Mr. Koch was called upon, and at a word he subscribed $5,000,

4

with the remark: "This I give you—but if the United States wants a frigate, I will build one for her myself!"

I knew him personally, and have often seen him at the northeast corner of Ninth and Market streets, where he resided for many years. In 1796, however, he lived at No. 263 South Front street.

In 1819 he removed to Paris, France, where he paid the great debt of nature on the 2d of July, 1830, in the 70th year of his age.

Willings & Francis occupied Nos. 21 and 23 Penn street above, on the north side of Lombard alley. The Willings's were father and son; and the elder, Thomas Willing, was the first president of the original United States Bank, chartered in 1791, under the administration of General Washington.

The parties of the mercantile firm were of the most respectable, and of the *elite* of that community. They were shipping merchants of the first class, extensively engaged in the East India and China trade, from and long after 1796, of which Thomas W. Francis was the spur—a man of enterprise and force—whilst Thomas M. Willing was the rein, or perhaps, qualifying medium; both, however, eminent men, as well as merchants of celebrity.

In the rear of James Forten's sail-loft, at No. 11 Penn street, in 1797, M. H. Messchert was also an eminent Hollander in the German trade. He was successful in his business, and retired with a very handsome competency.

This old gentleman enjoyed the run of his business with the hum of his musical genius; and in his retirement, put in practice the spark that awaited the leisure moment for ignition—for it is said of him, that he became a scholar of the violin after the run of his 60th year.

He certainly was a musical man—the concerts of the

Musical Fund Society seldom missed him, since he and his son, our cotemporary of No. 1224 Chestnut street, invariably patronized the efforts of that society.

Mr. M. seemed to have a very proper view of bringing up a child, in making his son his companion as much as possible. He died in December, 1833, in the 70th year of his age. He was the brother-in law of Jacob Gerard Koch, and cotemporary with him in trade.

Of mercantile interest, nothing here offers but that of Samuel Rhodes, who was a merchant at the south-east corner of Penn and Pine street.

In this compass there was a certain Daniel Dolby, whom I presume to have been a brother of *Joseph* Dolby, the very important sexton of Christ Church.

This *Joseph* Dolby was that dignitary in 1799, and for many years after, and was notorious for his identity with that church.

He was dignified and authoritative; took his seat at the entrance from the steeple; punctilious in his duties to the venerable Bishop or his aids in service; but his care of quiet during the prerequisites to the sermon, was very often marred by his "pish"—so long and so loud, that the chancel itself must have felt the breach of quiet due to its position.

But Mr. Dolby must have been a good timeist; for his measure of sermonizing liberated the chair in the steeple, whilst he relaxed his position by a walk to the wharf, but always back in time for the "Amen" of the pulpit.

May the reader pardon this *interregnum*, for if Mr. Dolby was not of the *mercantile* community, he certainly belonged to the ecclesiological; and as such, belonged to the life and doings of the olden time.

The intermediate space from Nixon's wharf to Wharton's

estate, gives nothing for note; but the diagram shows the appurtenances, and the occupants who have been already noticed in the preceding chapter.

Nixon & Walker, however, were shipping merchants, having their counting-house opposite to their wharf. Henry Nixon was president of the Bank of North America twenty years ago; and his father, John Nixon, before that.

CHAPTER IX.

PENN street ceases at Pine street, and Little Water street
stops at Lombard Alley; but Water street proper begins
between the two, and continues direct north to Callowhill
and beyond it.

The first object of note on Water street proper, is the well-
known and once opulent Joseph Sims, who was the active
mercantile business life of the northeast corner of Pine and
Water streets, and who built, owned, and occupied the first
and second block in the row north of the corner. His counting-house was about one hundred feet from the corner, where
he resided in the paternal mansion.

His wharf and dock below was the harbor of several of the
largest class of ships out of the port of Philadelphia, whose
successive and various cargos of teas and other East India
luxuries, heralded his enterprise in the manifold grocery
stores of our city, as they told of the "Woodrop Sims," the
"Rebecca Sims," the "Fame," and others of his ownership.

In addition to these, his landed possessions were extensive
collateral evidences of his increase.

He built, owned and lived in a first-class three-story brick
mansion, next below St. Peter's church, Third below Pine,
where he was resident in 1796. Subsequently he built the

extensive establishment, southwest corner of Ninth and Chestnut, at that time the pride of that street; whilst our present Laurel Hill was his country domains, and seat of retirement at will from the busy hum of city life. This country-seat contained twenty acres, besides ten acres on the opposite or east side of the Ridge Road, and are now the grounds of the Protestant Episcopal Church of St. James the Less.

But, alas! strong as his mountain, the stronger current of adversity swept it even to the valley of humiliation, and the crisis of 1823 gave his possessions to other owners.

Personally, he was none the worse for that; venerability gave tone to his respectability; and the real tone and character of Mr. Joseph Sims sparkled from his gentlemanly mien, even to his latest day.

He was the uncle of Mrs. E. S. Bird, of Ninth and Chestnut, into whose hands that estate fell.

The rest of his property was scattered by, and to his creditors, and left him destitute for many years; but before his close of life, he was absolved of the penalty of poverty, by befitting returns to his waning years.

Mr. Sims was of medium stature, and even in his decline very active, which doubtless shone to the full in his prime, when, besides his mercantile pursuits, he took an active part in public life.

He was a director of the first United States Bank, and one of the trustees of its *finale;* and a member of the Vestry of St. Peter's church, for sixty years, etc., etc., all which he filled with honor to himself, and satisfaction to his compeers.

He departed this life on the 29th of September, 1851, in the 91st year of his age, and was buried in the ground of St. Peter's church, corner of Third and Pine streets.

Joseph Johnson's ship-chandlery store was next above Mr. Sims's property, but in the line northward nothing of mercantile interest offers for note. The space was filled with boarding-houses, tailor-shops, cooper-shops, etc., all doubtless respectable in their calling; but being outside of my purpose, I must pass them with this respectful apology.

Fifty years ago, and long after, the house of Snowden & North was amongst the most prominent of ship-chandler establishments, occupying the premises next below the corner of Spruce street, through to the wharf, in front of Levi Hollingsworth & Son's dock and stores, numbered 2 and 3 in the diagram.

Mr. Hollingsworth gave active life to his wharf privileges, as one of the most extensive flour merchants in the city.

The Water street half of the corner of Water and Spruce, was a boarding-house; but the eastern part on the wharf, was occupied as the counting-house of Jesse & Robert Waln, in command of the wharf in front.

Jesse & Robert Waln were extensively engaged in European business, and being owners of many ships, had regularly one or more in the London trade. After the death of Jesse, Robert engaged in the China trade, which he pursued successfully for many years, and subsequently retired to the presidency of the Philadelphia Insurance Office.

Having entered into the character and standing of the occupants of this square, as they presented themselves on the Wharves, and inasmuch as they generally represented themselves at both points, I might pass the line by a mere reference to the diagram; but there was a nook on the wharf, and in connection with this line of Water-street occupants, of more than ordinary interest.

The counting-house of Robert Ralston, next above Ross's

wharf, was a source of disinterested benevolence, as well as extensive mercantile operations.

Mr. Ralston was one of the most extensive and successful merchants in the China trade, in Philadelphia.

He was a gentleman in all respects; a man of great integrity and probity, and of consistent practical piety in the Church, always bringing his Christianity to bear upon the temporal duties of his various relations in life. He was a man "blessed in his deed," influencing a kindred blessing of the life of charity over and amongst his brethren in the flesh.

The minutiæ of the character and doings of Mr. Ralston is beyond my reach and my purpose here; but my own personal knowledge of him was of a goodly sort.

He was a very fine-looking, full-sized, well-built person, of very gentlemanly manners, easy and entirely free of unnecessary reserve; a very valuable and efficient member of the Arch-street Presbyterian church, under the administration of Doctors Green and Janeway.

Mr. Ralston died on the 11th of August, 1836, in the 75th year of his age, and was buried on Saturday, the 13th, in the Presbyterian ground, Arch above Fifth street.

CHAPTER X.

Water street continued—Walnut to Chestnut—Site of the Mariner's Church
—Samuel Allen—Isaac Hazlehurst—Reed & Ford—John Wilcox—John
Welch—Charles Massey—Eyre & Massey—Ancestry of Charles Massey.

THE north-east corner of Water and Walnut streets was
the grocery store of Alexander Todd in 1795, and Robert
Corry, a wine merchant, was next above.

The Mariner's Church now fills the site of the earlier location of Samuel Allen, a merchant—subsequently of the
north side of Arch street, old No. 29.* Matthias Keely, merchant, afterward of No. 61 Race street, above Second street,
and Reed & Ford, all adjoining, and giving mercantile life to
the plot sixty years ago; but seventy years ago, 1789, Isaac
Hazlehurst did an extensive shipping business on and from
this spot.

Mr. Hazlehurst afterward built up the south-east corner
of Second and Drinkers alley, a very handsome two-story

---

* This was a mansion of the first class, twenty-five feet front, large front
entrance with columns and pediment finish, afterward occupied by Ambrose
Vass, counting-house and dwelling. It is now the property of Doctor William
Curran, who has recently remodeled the lower front and made a capacious
store, which now bears the No. 115, and is occupied by R. S. Reed & Co.,
wholesale grocers, being the first tenants under the new arrangement.

The altering of this front, with the new corner below, completely nullifies
the identity of old Arch street.

brick, some thirty feet front, and had his counting-house in the rear.

The counting-house of John Wilcox and his son Richard, occupied the south corner of Tun alley to the wharf.

Next above Tun alley we have the dwelling and counting-house of Mr. John Welsh, the sire in paternity and the root in mercantile pursuit of the present firm of S. & W. Welsh, of No. 50 South Wharves, a highly respectable and thrifty concern from root to branch.

Mr. John Welsh was a pioneer in these parts, having been already, in 1786, an apprentice in the counting-house of Joseph Russel, a prominent shipping merchant of that day.

After his servitude here, and a voyage to Port au Prince as supercargo, he entered the counting-house as clerk of Robert Ralston, another distinguished merchant of 1793, whose business he conducted during Mr. Ralston's absence, to his entire satisfaction.

In 1794, he entered the arena of mercantile strife on his own account, and by his skill and industry won the prize, even a competency for retirement, by the year 1806.

The war of 1812, however, started his energies; and at its close he again assumed the mantle of mercantile dignity—I say mercantile dignity, because he was *au fait* at all points—a good helmsman, without fear or favor, and governed his bark to a haven of peace, rest and comfort. He retired to his satisfaction, having established an enviable reputation as a merchant, renowned as the owner of many vessels, and popular far beyond the confines of the United States—and planted a succession to his thrifty character and standing, even now existing, in the firm of S. & W. Welsh, as before stated.

But he was more than all this—seeing that in 1803 he was one of the originators of the Philadelphia Bank, of which he

John Welsh
22 May 1849

was a director to the time of his death. Two of our insurance offices, also, owe their existence to his influence and efforts. But he was a philanthropist, and had the reputation, by practical observation, of being a "friend in need" —as ready to aid as to advise.

Having gradually relinquished his fond pursuit, and sold his last ship, he said to his consort of threescore years— "Now I have no ship!" She replied: "And soon you will have no wife!" To which he answered: "Then soon I shall have no self!" It was so; two short weeks ended their career! They departed not far asunder—an affecting but a most happy issue from time to eternity; for Mr. Welsh was not only a great merchant, but a good Christian.

He died on March 5th, 1854, at the full age of eighty-four years.

Although Mr. Welch was well-known and popular with all of us of his day, it behooves me to give credit to the "Enquirer" of the 6th of March, 1854, for the minutiæ of this notice, which I am happy to endorse, as well from my own knowledge as from earlier contemporaneous testimony.

Joseph R. Evans took the foot-print of Mr. Welsh, purchasing his store of No. 31; and in or near 1807, held forth here under the firm, first, of Welsh, Maris & Evans—Mr. Welsh permitting his name as a pioneer in the trade; second, under the firm of Maris & Evans; thirdly, 1818, as Joseph R. Evans—when and where he became eminent as a shipping merchant, particularly in the London trade with his ships "Electra" and "Thames"—and deservedly popular as a citizen and gentleman in good standing. He was brought up in the counting-house of Nixon & Walker; and in his heyday was a codirector with Mr. Welsh in the Philadelphia bank for many years.

His demise was sudden and unexpected; an attack of heart disease having closed his existence in a business visit in New York, where he departed this life on the 8th of September, 1848, in the sixty-sixth year of his age; being even then in the full tide of life.

The counting-house of Thomas Lloyd, of Market street, and Wm. Sykes, intervening, brings us to the store and counting-house of Eyre & Massey; of this firm our Mr Charles Massey of No. 170 Arch street, now eighty-one years of age, is the survivor.

The tenure of this gentleman's existence leads us far into the last century; and, thanks to him and his tenacious memory, gives me an antiquarian scope.

Mr. Massey was brought up in the counting-house of Henry Pratt, who, in 1795, took into partnership his earlier clerk, Mr. Abraham Kintzing.

This association links him to the times and doings of 1795 With an inquiring mind peeping into antecedents, and as such losing nothing of his training nor yet of his observation.

After a servitude of four years, 1795–1799, with Pratt & Kintzing, he formed a connection with his brother and Thomas Shoemaker; and under the firm of Masseys & Shoemaker, conducted a West India and a coasting trade at and from No. 24 South Wharves.

In 1803, Mr. Manuel Eyre became his partner—and the well-known firm of Eyre & Massey of No. 23 South Water street and No. 28 South Wharves, where maritime facilities found a response to their offerings, and the East and West Indies, as well as Europe and South America, knew them as the life of busy scenes for forty-two years, without blur or blemish, to the death of Mr. Eyre in 1845, which of course, dissolved the connection.

As matter of curiosity as well as history, I append here
the world-wide route of their operations, furnished to me by
Mr. Charles Massey, the survivor of the firm; there being
nothing, perhaps, on record to surpass it, at least in Philadelphia.

First. They owned during their business connection, upward of twenty sail of vessels, from the largest size of ships
down to schooners, calculated for the various ports of their
destination.

Second. Their enterprise reached the following ports: Arch-
angel, Tòningen, Hamburg, Amsterdam, Antwerp, Havre,
Bordeaux, Bayonne, Lisbon, St. Ubes, Oporto, Cadiz, St.
Lucar, St. Sebastian, Gibraltar, Malaga, Barcelona, Marseilles,
Island of Sardinia, Genoa, Leghorn, Palermo, Cette, London,
Liverpool, Ireland, Plymouth, Falmouth, Madeira, Teneriffe,
Cape de Verd Islands, Vera Cruz, Alvarado, Jamaica, St.
Jago de Cuba, Havana, New Providence, St. Domingo, St.
Thomas, Guadaloupe, St. Croix, Curaçoa, Laguira, Mara-
caibo, Cayenne, Pernambuco, Corunna in Spain, Bahia, Rio de
Janeiro, Santos, Rio Grande, Paranaquay—the last seven ports
on the coast of Brazil. Buenos Ayres, Montevideo, Valparaiso,
Irico, Coquimbo, Copiapo, Lima, Guayaquil, Panama, the last
seven around Cape Horn. Sandwich Islands, Java, Sumatra,
Manilla, Canton, Calcutta, Madras, besides some dozen ports
in the United States.

Third. One of their ships, the "Globe," made eight voyages
to China and back. This ship, during a period of twenty
years made twenty-nine voyages, some of them of more than
one year's duration.

Fourth. It is a remarkable fact, that in all this risk and
adventure, they never made a total loss.

It belongs to the history of this firm to say, that although so extensively engaged in mercantile pursuits, they devoted a part of their time to public service.

Mr. Massey was for many years a member of the Select Council of our city, and in turn, also of the Common Council, in which he took an active part. He was chairman of the committee on opening Delaware Avenue, agreeably to the will of Stephen Girard, in 1834; also, appointed by the Court of Quarter Sessions a juror of valuation of the wharf fronts; and for his general knowledge of wharf property, selected as chairman of that jury. And he, with his fellow-jurors, did value by critical arithmetical estimate, the property required for the avenue from Arch to Chestnut, and from Walnut to the lower side of Spruce street,—being owner of part of the intermediate square, he was ineligible for that duty.

Mr. Manuel Eyre, who was also brought up in the counting-room of Henry Pratt, was no less energetic or public-spirited. He was a member of our City Council, and a director of the United States Bank of 1816, and again of the same under the charter of Pennsylvania of 1836; but his forte was more that of an agriculturist, to which he devoted mainly the last twenty years of his life, being the owner and operator of two farms near the city, and three in the State of Delaware—indeed a very projector of Delaware City.

Mr. Eyre was of full size, being six feet in height, square built and well proportioned—he had an independent but not a haughty carriage—he had a very prominent nose and strong features generally, with a thoughtful and observing eye, shaded by his hat of broader brim than fashion called for. He was a man of integrity and respectability, unmoved by any adverse crook in trade, or flow of incidental success.

He was the son of Manuel Eyre, Sen., of Kensington, an

eminent shipwright there, who had been a Colonel in the Revolutionary war of 1776, and subsequently a member of the Legislature of Pennsylvania.

There being no shade nor shadow of a likeness of my subject, I offer the description as a substitute for a portrait that else should be here.

A curious feature of the times was that they insured, frequently, to any part of the world, *by the year*, with liberty of proceeding to any port without notice.

I give this—neither as puff, nor boast for the principals—but as appears to me a very extraordinary tissue of mercantile force, and equally so of successful issues, ignorant of a parallel, and well assured that we have no such expansive minds nowadays, nor courage for the opportunities if they even were open. Our capitalists live, move and operate under the smoke of their own chimneys, and hold too much to the penny and the cake too.

The natural business capacity of the survivor has lost nothing by the demise of his partner—his habits, impelled by the freshness of his mind, continues the life of his activity; so that even now, the elbow-chair of his early haunt embraces him daily to foster his ruminations through the pleasures and the pains of his threescore years association.

But a tribute is due to the elasticity of his mind, memory, and understanding. His mind, unworn by time, with a memory even pentagraphic, gives intelligence to his mental issues and authenticity to his historical reference. As an evidence, permit the following. In my search for dots and lines of the past, especially the wharves, I called on Mr. M., who at once gave me a diagram of several squares, which being compared with an original draft made by Reading Howell, more than fifty years ago, and copy taken by my very valu able friend and help in this matter, Mr. E. F. Durang, an architect of value, was found to be correct to a line.

Mr. M. is an antiquarian to all intents and purposes, and holds valuable statistics of our city of more than sixty years gathering. Although not a birthright member, he has always been an adherent to the Society of Friends, and a regular attendant of their meetings of worship; his ancestors being of that faith, and he, an early pupil of the Friends' school in Philadelphia.

He is an Irishman by root, his great grandfather, Samuel Massey, having emigrated hither from Ireland, in the year 1699, the time of William Penn.

As the son of Samuel Massey, and grandson of Wight Massey, both shipping merchants, all of the last century, he has fallen heir to some old time affairs, amongst which he has a lease of his grandfather, Wight Massey, merchant, to Robert Dixon, for a lot of ground, described as being at the northwest corner of Arch and Broad streets, containing ninety-nine feet on Arch, by three hundred and six feet on Broad street, to a vacant lot, through which now Cherry street passes.

The lease is dated March 25th, 1749, term seven years, at £4, Pennsylvania currency, $10 67 per annum, payable half-yearly.

This lot now holds the First Baptist church, and one of its most valuable members, Mr. Thomas Watson, who built and resides next west of the church edifice.

Besides the above venerable relic, Mr. Massey is in possession of the receipt book of his great grandfather, Samuel Massey, of 1699; all the mercantile books of his grandfather, as also those of his father, Samuel Massey, 1754 to 1778.

CHAPTER XI.

In 1795, John Skyren, merchant, occupied the northeast
corner of Water and Chestnut street, and John Little was his
neighbor; but previously, in 1793, the Chestnut street part
of this block, at No. 5, was occupied by Joseph Anthony &
Son, shipping merchants, of considerable note of that day,
and John Maybin afterward.

This Joseph Anthony was the father of the Joseph
Anthony, Jr., of No. 94 Market street, a notable silversmith,
well known a few doors above Third street, on the south
side.

His senior, the elder Mr. Anthony, built and occupied the
large three-story brick house, northeast corner of Ninth and
Market streets; the house afterward the residence of Jacob
Gerard Koch, heretofore noticed.

The stores and counting-house of the Messrs. Anthony &
Son, with the lots belonged to the Pemberton estate.

John Stille, Jr., and Benjamin & Samuel Stille, occupied
the store next above, as commission merchants, as agents in
part of the celebrated William Gray, of Salem, Mass., for the
sale of his various India and China goods.

5

Willis & Yardley occupied the next above as a flour store 1802.

Thomas Pryor, next above, was the brother of Norton Pryor, a well-known extensive dealer in, and importer of, hides; they were the uncles of our Charles Massey.

Charles Massey, another uncle of our venerable Charles, a merchant of some account, was located the second house above Crooked Billet Alley, in 1788.

Buckridge Sims, a brother of Joseph Sims, occupied the store and counting-house next above as a shipping merchant; and here adjoining we have the busy and thrifty quarters of our prominent, and in process of time, opulent and valuable citizen, Paul Beck, Jr.

After serving his time with Henry Sheaf, at the southeast corner of Market and Fifth streets, in the grocery business, we find him a fixture, in 1789, in the same trade, on his own account, where in due time he increased his borders from No. 11 to Nos. 11, 12 and 15, where the firm of Beck & Harvey was formed, and flourished for some years, until the retirement of Mr. Harvey to private life, Mr. Beck pursuing the tide of fortune till age and physical inability set his perseverance at nought, but leaving opulence for his reward, and a heart fraught with active benevolence.

The day of his mercantile enterprises was as well, in him, a focus of public spirit.

In the year 1820, he suggested and proposed a plan to improve the river front from the wharf to Front street, but failed of like spirits to carry out the idea.

The annexed plan will show the features of the project, from which we may draw the following conclusions:—

To describe the changes and proposed improvements, as submitted by him to the City Councils, in 1820, we may first

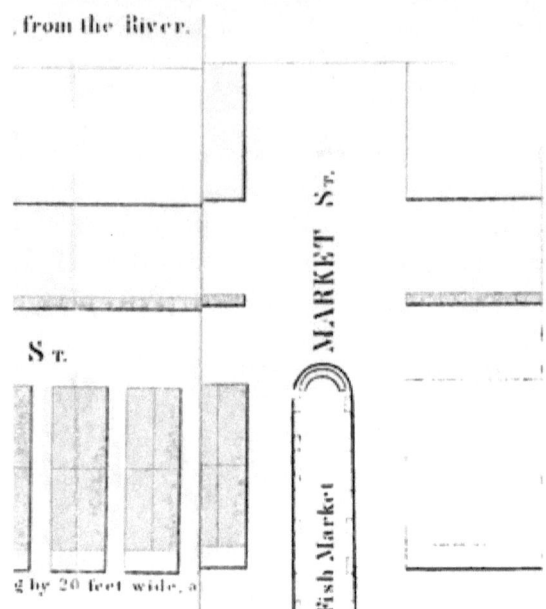

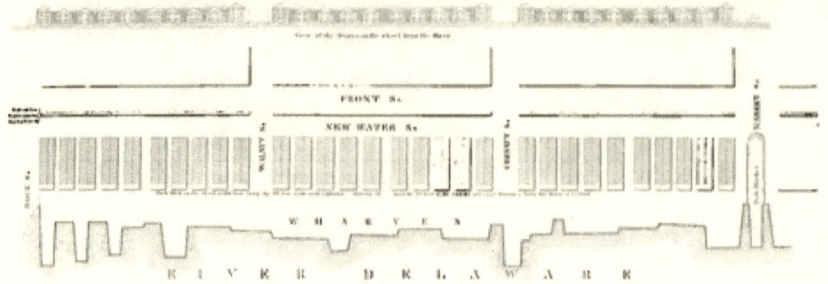

6

1

I
b

)
r

s
t
e

speak of the plan, the most important feature of which was, to vacate the property on the east side of Front street, and build a retaining wall on the street line, capped with an iron railing, and create a new Water street on the eastern or lower side of the wall, and removing all the then present existing buildings, laying out the vacated ground in new, uniform building blocks, each forty feet front by one hundred feet in depth, each block being subdivided into four store-houses, having a cartway between every block, the front on Delaware Avenue being set back from the wharf line seventy-five feet on the average.

The range of buildings represents a geometrical elevation of the buildings, the retaining wall and its railing showing in between the several blocks at the cartways.

The extent of the improvement was to be from Vine to Spruce street, and the estimated cost, $3,651,000.

To say the least, the idea was as interesting as it was bold, and could it have been carried out, would have made the port of Philadelphia and its embankment, perhaps, the most picturesque in the world.

He built the first shot-tower in the United States; it was situated on the north side of Arch street, near the Schuylkill, and paid well for the enterprise.

Mr. Beck was the architect of his own fortune, which was great, and well applied in public benefactions.

He was amongst the founders of the Sunday School Union, which, with many other public charities, he endowed handsomely and substantially by his last will and testament.

He was rather small of stature, very neat in person, of mild, modest, and benevolent countenance, marked by a bearded wart near his chin—rather interesting than otherwise—a gentleman in manners, and active in business matters.

His residence in 1805, and for many years, was a very handsome first-class three-story brick mansion, on the north side of Market street above Eighth—old number, 315. The lot extended to Filbert street three hundred and six feet, and in width on Market street was thirty-three feet. In his decline, he had an office in the rear of his dwelling, over the door of which he had the *original* sign of Paul Beck, Jr.

The house was built by the Rev. Samuel Magaw, rector of St. Paul's Church, and the predecessor of our late venerable Dr. Pilmore.

The premises were sold at public auction in December, 1849, and bought by Freed, Ward & Freed, for $16,500, and is now a flour mart and railroad depot.

Paul Beck died December 22d, 1844, in the eighty-fourth year of his age.

Petit & Bayard were parties in mercantile interests as next neighbors of Mr. Beck, and Rumford Daws gave mercantile life to the premises above, whilst Negus's Ferry was doubtless the busiest, and perhaps the most noisy life of the neighborhood.

Jacob Clement & Bankson Taylor were extensive grocers next above, 1795.

Bankson Taylor, after retiring from the grocery business, became a mariner for a season, and commanded the ship "Gleaner" to Calcutta in 1808. After his experience here, he again entered the mercantile list on shore, in company with Samuel Allen of Arch street, where the firm of Allen & Taylor was prominent in 1817. In 1823, he was alone in business, and had his counting-house on Bickley's wharf, above Market street.

His partners were highly respectable; but Mr. Clement was the plainer man of the three. Capt. Taylor left a handsome estate in very good hands, and Mr. Clement a good business with very respectable sons to attend to it.

The life of the corner, however, was in our well and wide known William Newel, who was identified here as a popular grocer from the year 1792, and for many years into the present century.

He was succeeded by his son William, conducting the same business; and even now, *his* son William C. perpetuates the memory of his grandfather in like pursuits, next below the homestead on the same soil, where also the sign of his original of 1792 shows forth the date of the busy point of the life of the grandsire, and the root of the third generation in the same trade on the same spot.

It may not be amiss to charge history here with a fixture of more than fifty years' growth, on the opposite southwest corner of Market and Water streets.

John Culin betokened his calling as tailor and vendor of ready-made clothing there, already in 1808; and even yet holds the spot in continuance of his calling.

Mr. Culin is therefore now a venerable relic of the olden time, and holds his own as a respectable and good citizen.

Since writing the above, Mr. Culin has been gathered to his fathers.

He died, it is said, of apoplexy, on the 27th of July, 1859, in the eighty-third year of his age.

About midway, around the corner toward the wharf, we must notice *en passant* the Blue Anchor Tavern, kept by John Michaeljohn: a famous resort for the boatmen and fishermen of that day.

CHAPTER XII.

Water street—Market to Arch—Bohl Bohlen—B. & J. Bohlen—Thomas Leiper
—Louis Croussilat—Stephen Girard—His mansion—S. V. Anderson—Crooke
Stevenson—G. & H. Calhoun—Samuel Crawford—Smith & Wood—Smith &
Ridgway—Job Butcher—Robeson & Paul—John Clark.

IN passing this square, although I have material to dot and
line every one of its tennants, I cannot diverge too much
from my intent and purpose, without trespassing upon a com-
piler of a Directory, and must therefore confine myself to the
permanence and prominence of its mercantile life.

In 1793, Bohl Bohlen, a Hollander, was known as merchant at No. 7 North Water street. He, perhaps, was the first
importer and vendor of "Weesp Anchor Gin" in Philadelphia. In 1797-8, his brother John, his clerk theretofore,
became his partner, and B. & J. Bohlen still were at No. 7
North Water street. In 1802 this firm was known at No. 26
Chestnut street; but subsequently, 1805, at Nos. 67 and 69
South Fourth street, where death dissolved and finally annihilated the firm after a most successful pursuit to the end of
the business term of both members of the firm.

They were both good specimens of Holland merchants,
first class, real business men, and stemming all the crosses
and crooks of more than half a century of active business
life, dissolved *sine die*, leaving a very extensive evidence of
their successful labors in an unmistakable balance in their
favor.

Our old familiar citizen, Thomas Leiper, in the year 1795, found himself at home at No. 9, next above the Messrs. Bohlen, where he may have began his dealings in snuff and tobacco.

Mr. Leiper was an eminent tobacconist, subsequently on the south side of Market street above Eighth street, where the statue of a Scotch laddie at the door, in the act of taking a pinch of snuff, silently but significantly announced the sale of snuff, tobacco, and cigars within, whilst the proprietor was known in his *sortie* by his measured and independent gait, and his fanciful neck gear of a red bandanna handkerchief, drawn around from the back of his neck, folding the ends under his vest, showing the red border, and ever and anon signalizing Thomas Leiper; which permit me to say, was not without its effect upon his very respectable appearance.

Louis Croussilat ranged prominently in this row, No. 13 being his residence; immediately back of this, Croussilat's wharf and counting-house were well-known. Mr. Croussilat was a French merchant, in the French trade, extensively and favorably known as a shipping merchant, 1802. After retiring from his mercantile pursuits, he purchased and resided on a small farm in the Neck, below the city, known as "Point Breeze," on the river Schuylkill, since sold to the city by his only survivor, a daughter, for the erection of city gas-works.

Joseph Carson, the grandsire of our present fellow-citizens. Hugh L. Carson, a merchant on Chestnut street, and Doctor Joseph Carson, of No. 1120 Spruce street, was a prominent merchant at No. 7, before Mr. Bohlen, 1785 to 1791.

But there was a speck of the "wealth of nations" in this Water-street line; the universally-known Stephen Girard was a meteor of the mercantile community, at No. 23.

He was celebrated for his perseverance, indefatigable

industry, economy, and almost unparalleled success in all his undertakings. Every thing he touched seemed to turn to gold. He was, in effect, a very philosopher's stone.

It is said of him, that he did not begin his increase until he was forty years of age—encouraging to early unsuccessful strife, and a beacon to perseverance, and the changes and chances of life.

In 1791, Mr. Girard kept a greengrocery and provision store at No. 43 North Front street, occupying through to and on Water-street, at No. 31, where he lived and moved carefully and economically in all his domestic arrangements. An old lady, who lived with him as seamstress to his wife at this early period of his life, has often told me, that neither he, she, nor they, were ever allowed to indulge in more edibles than was absolutely necessary. He therefore set out to make money, and fortune beset him, and wealth surrounded him.

From a tablet on the balcony of the second story of his subsequent residence, at No. 23 North Water-street, it may be fairly inferred that he built and occupied that domain in 1796.

This house was a four-story pressed brick of the first-class, in which his counting-house was the front room, on Water street. The adjoining room in the rear was his breakfast and dining-room, which was smaller than the counting-room, being narrowed by the staircase in the entry.

The parlor was the front room (on Water-street) of the second story, and his chief clerk, Mr. John A. Barclay, says, was handsomely furnished with ebony chairs and cushioned seats covered with velvet, and sofas to match. The bed-chambers were in the rear and above this parlor.

He had a private counting-room next below, keeping the

lower floor as his sanctum, whilst the floor above was the depository of his books and papers.

I am thus particular about his dwelling, because our city Fathers have obliterated his whereabouts, annihilated his business identity, and have sunk their memoirs in the Girard Estate, with small thanks to the donor, destroying every vestige of the means that begat the misnomer of his intentions; a misappropriation of his fund, that he, Stephen Girard, would repudiate and denounce, were he here present.

I have nothing to do with the private character of Mr. Girard. I am aware that much has been charged upon his want of affection to his wife; but Mr. Barclay, before mentioned, tells me that, as he lay a corpse, a Mr. and Mrs. Price came to see it, whereupon Mrs. Price, his wife's sister, said, "There lies one of the best of husbands." Mr. Barclay being an eye and ear-witness to the scene, is certainly good authority. And as "good may always be said of the dead," let the memory of Girard have the benefit of this.

But more, Mr. Girard, despite reports to the contrary, was certainly imbued with a spirit of benevolence, but guided by prudence, and regulated by his own peculiar views of propriety: for instance, a man once went to him for alms or employment. Girard set him to work to remove a pile of bricks from one side of his yard to the other; the man soon reported the job as done. Mr. Girard said, "Now carry them back again." The man did so, and again reported, "Done, sir." Girard again said, "Now put them back to where you found them." The employee demurred and declined. Mr. Girard said, "Ha! you do not want work," and paid him. This was his idea of promoting industry.

Again, it was a tangible fact to see the large gate on Eleventh below Market street, of Dunlap's lot, thrown open in the winter season for the benefit of the poor; for whom he had accumulated, on that lot, the refuse lumber from his various buildings, from which the humble hearth often was made to glow with grateful aspirations to the thoughtful donor.

And again, much as he was said to be opposed to religion, he constantly did give to the raising of "holy temples," but he chose to measure his donation; but dictation to liberality was a dangerous experiment, and a negative most certainly followed the most familiar effort.

But most of all, he winds up his life by a grand scheme for the benefit of our race; and however his views have been misconstrued, and his means wasted in the execution of his benevolent purpose, the heart and the sympathy of Girard, must forever be felt by the manifold recipients of his bounty.

I do not herald these as emanations from any religious principles—for he had no credit for any—but rather as a moral principle always directed to the well-being of his fellow-man.

The love of gain was doubtless a cardinal point with him; but it was an impulse to his enterprise, and the argument to his courage, for he was a merchant of skill and of liberal and extensive views.

He was the first merchant in Philadelphia, and perhaps in the United States, that some fifty years ago undertook to lengthen a ship by cutting her in two, and inserting twenty or thirty feet in her middle, in view of increasing her capacity and her speed. The experiment was successfully performed by his ship-carpenter, Isaac White.

Preparatory to the operation, the ship was placed in a cradle, or ways, and hauled up on the shore by large cables attached to capstans, as performed on his ship "Liberty," and another of his ships, afterward.

But employment of purse as well as person, was another cardinal point with him, and armed his enterprising spirit to grapple with the monetary world.

To this end he purchased the old United States Bank building, and established there, in 1812, a banking institution, under the name of the "Girard Bank," appointing George Simpson cashier,[*] and himself acting as president. This was another successful branch of his fertile conceptions; but the notoriety of this original "Girard Bank" is stereotyped to the world, and needs—from me—no more than the reference to it as connected with its originator.

I am not here to extenuate his faults, nor to denounce his errors. I knew him as good to the poor, and kindly indulgent to the sick, of which the Yellow Fever of 1793 and 1798 bore ample testimony; but I knew him also, as a reputed debtor to Christianity, notwithstanding he was a liberal contributor to the building of churches.

An incident in his mercantile life, showing his ready wit, may not be without interest in closing this memoir.

He had a cargo of salt at his wharf, at which his principal dealer in that article—to cheapen it to his own price—shied. Girard's *jeu d'esprit* was prompt to corner his antagonist.

"Tom," said he to his porter, "why can't you buy that cargo?" Tom laughed, and replied, "Why, sir, how can I buy? I have no money." "Never mind," said Girard, "you can buy it for all. Take it and sell it by the load, and pay me as you sell it." The porter took the hint. The salt was out of the market—his opponents were foiled—and Tom,

---

[*] After the death of Mr. Simpson, Joseph Roberts was his cashier until his death, and the winding up of the bank. Mr. Roberts was one of his executors.

from this hit, became a prominent salt merchant, and as such flourished for many years after.

> "A man of skill he was, with all his faults,
> Subject to like returns, or Wit's assaults;
> And tho' in vision blurr'd, in glance he peer'd,
> And saw the germ that others miss'd or fear'd."

Stephen Girard was married in 1777, to Mary Lumm, by the Rev. Samuel Magaw, Rector of St. Paul's Church.

Samuel V. Anderson was a grocer, and resident at No. 25, next above Girard, in and long after 1802.

North & Haskins were also in the full tide of the grocery trade near by, at No. 31. This Mr. North was afterward High Sheriff of the City and County of Philadelphia.

Gustavus & Hugh Calhoun were equally prominent as shipping-merchants, in connection with their several Charleston packets, next above. This Gustavus Calhoun was the father-in-law of the late John Bohlen, and Hugh Calhoun was the son-in-law of the late, aged John M. Taylor.

Montgomery & Newbolds were perhaps the most popular wholesale grocers in this range. Mr. Montgomery was bland, free and unsophisticated in social, as well as in business life, and was popular for his accessibility.

The Messrs. Newbold were from Mount Holly, of good character and standing, and good business men. William Newbold, of this firm, was the father of our active cotemporary, William H. Newbold, of Dock and Walnut, a very lively specimen of a spirited ancestry somewhere.

These gentlemen, with their families, were, most of them, resident over their stores or counting-houses.

The houses were of the first class, well built, and handsomely finished in the interior, with broad, open newell stairways, guarded by broad oaken hand-rail, leading to the upper apartments; the parlors being in the second story, with an unobstructed view of the Delaware and its floating wealth. These parlors were handsomely finished with carved mantels, and some fancy work on the ceiling.

Water-street being the Court end of the town in the days hereunto referred, taste and genius in constructing habitations were as active and lively in proportion to the population, as they are even now; their tastes and genius were students of their comfort, subject to the economy of life, and they lived better and at less cost than their equals of the present day.

The lower story and rear front were the counting-houses and stores of the merchants resident above. Wood-sheds and lumber-nooks were humble incumbents of the yards on the wharf beneath the windows of the counting-houses; and even now I see the burly negro, at full length, sunning himself on the shed of Montgomery & Newbolds, alarming us boys by a single stir, as we floundered in the basin of the "Broken Wharf," immediately under his eye.

As early as 1793, our well-known citizens, Elliston & John Perot, held forth, prominently and extensively, as wholesale merchants, at No. 41; but their domicils were side and side, at 297 and 299 Market street, north side, below Eighth street, where Edward Perot, the son of John Perot, remains as a notch in the so-called march of improvement.*

---

* Elliston Perot built his house in 1793, and John Perot built next door, in 1804.

Elliston Perot was married at Friends' Meeting, to Sarah, daughter of Samuel Sansom, of Front street; and John Perot was married by the Rev. Dr. Blackwell, to Miss Tyebout, daughter of Andrew Tyebout, of Chestnut street, hatter, 1783.

These sires were remarkable for their steady and unob-trusive walk in life. The one was a member of the Society of Friends, the other of the Episcopal church; but they were two that varied in opinion, and still agreed to differ.

They were in business together for many years, and died in the harness, at a good old age—as full of benefits as they were of years: they were good men and true.

Charles French and Samuel Crawford made up the line to the Old Ferry alley. Mr. French retired many years ago to private life, in Arch street, north side, near Seventh street; and as matter of further history, it may be in place to state that Mr. Crawford had the rearing of the late Joseph Harrison, Sr., in the grocery business—who died on the 9th of December, 1858, in his eighty-first year.

Joseph Harrison became the son-in-law of Mr. Crawford, and the father of our opulent cotemporary, Joseph Harrison, Jr., to whose credit be it recorded, that thus far he is none the worse for his vast estates.

Onward, above the Old Ferry alley, we had the extensive dealers in groceries, the firms of Smith & Wood, and Smith & Ridgway, in the same building, the latter having their rooms over the former. Success attended their operations, and they ultimately had something to show for their labors in business life.

Smith & Ridgway were largely engaged as shipping and importing merchants, in the West India and European trade. They owned many vessels, and at one time shipped largely to Antwerp, as far back as 1796.

They were successful in their trade; but Jacob Ridgway afterward settled in Antwerp as a merchant—had a large commission business—and after some years returned to Philadelphia with a very handsome reward of his mercantile prowess.

James Smith retired with ample means to quiet quarters; whilst Mr. Ridgway continued his business habits, guarding his accumulations till time to him was no longer, and departed this life on the 30th of May, 1843, in the seventy-fifth year of his age.

Mr. James Smith, of this firm, died on the 27th of May, 1826, in the sixty-sixth year of his age; a highly esteemed member of the Society of Friends.

Mr. Job Butcher, though a retail grocer, was a very respectable part of the active business life of No. 49, even in 1793, and for many years after—some distance into the present century.

Our neighbor Butcher was an indulgent patron of youth, whose good-nature elicited their familiarity and permitted access to his sugar-casks, whilst he winked at the resistless temptation at the ends of their fingers.

But we had the freedom of the store from front to rear, where, on the landing at the head of a flight of steps leading down to his yard and wharf, he had one or two pet Raccoons, with which, between school-hours, we were allowed to play to our heart's content; but the black lumps of his sugar, if even less attractive, was the appetital relish of our fun, leaving yet a sweet savor to the reminiscence.

He was a clever old gentleman, of the Society of Friends; was a kind neighbor—attended to his business—and finished his course unscathed of the evils of failure in his honest and laudable pursuits.

His son, Amos W., succeeded him; and, I believe, successfully.

He too was a ray of his father, retiring in manner, but steady and forceful in his matters of business.

The lineage continues in Front, near Race, No. 146, under the firm of Butcher & Brother, sons of Amos W., and grandsons of my old and familiar friend, Job Butcher; they occupy the site of the late Henry Pratt's dwelling.*

Robeson & Paul were identities of No. 53, and their extensive flour and provision store there was a wide-spread notoriety. They were there already in 1797, and for many years after.

The corner of Arch and Water, was the grocery store and residence of the Mr. John Clark heretofore noticed.

His brother, Mr. Jacob Clark, who had for his clerk our own Moses Kempton, the present, and for many years past, very valuable Accounting Warden of Christ Church, was the business grocer of next door below. Permit me to add here, that the Clark family were of the most respectable part of our community.

---

* Job Butcher died February, 1819, aged seventy-seven years; and his son Amos died in 1846, aged sixty-five years.

CHAPTER XIII.

Water street—Arch to Race—Isaac Austin, at the corner—Mrs. Burkhard—
Isaac Wainwright—William Peddle—Timothy Paxson—Latimer & Murdock
—J. Vanuxem—Steinmetz—Major Hodgdon—L. Huron—Goldsmith—Elder
—Summerl & Brown—Andrew Hodge—Dr. Hodge—Henry Pratt—Wilson,
Boat Builder—Rugan & Rhodes—James Crawford—John Warder & Son—
Harvey & Davis—Capt. Davis.

To this northeast corner of Arch and Water street, attaches
some notoriety, inasmuch as our late celebrated Com. Dale
was united here in the bonds of matrimony, to a niece of Isaac
Austin, then and there residing as a responsible watchmaker;
and in addition, a peep on the hill finds the early bell-ringer
of Christ Church, who practiced upon the octave in his garret,
in order to perfect his peals on Sunday; but, more important
still, next below him, sat our subsequent eminent Bays New-
combe, delving into Coke and Blackstone, founding a legal
reputation, which he attained in after life.

Leaving this point, the Widow Burkhard claims notice,
next to the corner on Water street, where she and her husband resided, No. 57, in 1793, and adjoins the industrial
block and pump-maker depot of Isaac Wainwright. These
premises run through to the wharf and the water itself, for at
the foot of his yard there was a dock for the soaking and
safe keeping of logs, a very sink of mortality to those who
ventured to run their role from wharf to wharf, a memorable
fact to your author, who, but for the timely hand of a larger

6

boy, and the extra capillary of his head, would certainly not have been here now to tell a tale of days and things *lang syne*.

Humbly, but vastly important to maritime requirements, the saw, the auger, and the chisel noised their daily services to shape and bore a pump, or fit a sheeve and block to the hand of an inquiring mariner.

Mr. Wainwright was perhaps the most popular block and pumpmaker of his day.

His son Jonathan succeeded him in the business, and continued it for many years. Thence he removed to Kensington, and established a saw-mill and board-yard, and at the same time acting as President of the Kensington Bank.

He resigned the presidency creditable to his services, and retired to his more active business calling, which, with his sons, he yet industriously pursues.

In this connection I take occasion to state, that his brother William was the persecuted President of the Commercial Bank : for upon investigation, he was honorably acquitted.

Isaac Wainwright, the sire, died in July, 1844, in his eighty-third year.

William Peddle was an oak cooper, next above, whose premises extended through to the wharf, north side of Wainwright's dock.

A public alley to the wharf, along the north side of Peddle's premises, could it speak, might tell of the battle-ground on the wharf, where belligerents met to settle disputes *vi et armis*, and gymnastic gyrations from the storm of their bosoms.

There were "bullies" in those days, who seemed to take pride in championship, some of whom of fair reputation I could revive here—but let their dotings, dottings and doings be ———! It was, however, battle-ground to which appointments were made, and upon which the ring of some depth hailed the victor, or bore the vanquished to quarters of peace, and repair of damage.

It must be observed here, however, that they were not prize fights, but more exuberances of skill and bravura than ebullitions of wrath: and all this sixty years ago!

Craving forbearance for this rude incident of the times, my return to Water street leads me to more respectable and more profitable doings.

At the upper corner of the alley here referred to, our well-known citizen, Timothy Paxson, bought, sold and delivered flour by the quantity.

Mr. Paxson was a staid, steady, plain Friend, wending his way, morning, noon and evening, from his dwelling at No. 81 Arch, north side, above Front street, to his long-standing haunt of No. 65 North Water street, before and long after 1802. In 1799, he resided at No. 16 Key's alley.

Latimer & Murdock were also prominent dealers in flour, next above Mr. Paxson, a very respectable house, in good business standing, and of desirable social relations.

Mr. Latimer—more especially known to me as a Christian gentleman—was a very neat and handsome man, medium height, stout, but well proportioned, and highly esteemed in Church and State.

In immediate connection in this line, we had John Steinmetz, Jr., a wholesale grocer, and Major Samuel Hodgdon, Superintendent of the Public Stores of the United States.

James Vanuxem, a rather small-sized, neat, and gentlemanly-looking man, was a merchant of some note, at the third door from the corner of the alley leading to the famous Red Stores, 1799; but afterward, in 1802, was located at No

186 Market street, next below General Washington's house, south side, near Sixth street.

The venerable William Smith was next resident at the upper corner of the alley, and was there also the opulent recipient of the profits of his West India plantations.

As a chain of family identity, I note that his memory is perpetuated in the Wager and the Huber family; Peter Wager having married a daughter of his son Stafford, and Tobias Huber, a daughter of *his* daughter, Mrs. (Doctor) Elder, of whom I am free to say here, that Mrs. Wager was a *beau ideal* of beauty in form and feature—one of the prettiest women of her day.

Doctor Elder was resident next above Mr. Smith, and assorted the tone of the neighborhood; but the mercantile operations of Summerl & Brown were next above, in bold relief, and their counting-house here, and the dwelling of Joseph Summerl next door, were marked points of their whereabouts.

They were prominent in mercantile life, and popular in that community.

Andrew Hodge was another of the fraternity of merchants near by; and again an "M. D.," in the person and profession of Hugh Hodge, assorted the respectability of the gathering here.

Here we reach the domicil of Henry Pratt, at No. 93, in 1795.

This was a first-class three-story brick house, with iron railing in front of the lower windows, with slab pave inside; the railing there was a defense against the too near approach of the many passing sailors.

An alley of twelve or fifteen feet separated the dwelling from the stores and counting-house of Pratt & Kintzing, at

No. 95, where Mr. Pratt and Pratt & Kintzing, had at their elbows the late Manuel Eyre, and my venerable friend, Charles Massey, as active assistants in the requirements of the counting-house.

The upper stories of the store—which was of four stories—crossed over the alley by an arch. The whole ground-plot was about sixty feet front on Water street.

A boat-building emporium diversified the field of mercantile doings; and John Wilson, the proprietor, enjoyed the benefits of his skill and the fruits of his labor. It was a popular resort for the lovers of aquatic sports.

Rugan & Rhodes were well-known shipping merchants on these premises, in 1809—after John Wilson.

Captain Rugan is still with us; and we reunite him to his occupation of fifty years ago, with all due respect, and thus revive his memory, and that of his early associates, to by-gone days.

James Crawford, another shipping merchant, adjoined the above, on the north, in 1798; but in 1806, John Warder & Sons continued the mercantile life and spirit of this spot.

The corner of Race and Water streets was the ship-chandlery of Harvey & Davis.

Mr. Harvey was unknown to me; but Captain Davis still lives in my memory, as a well-dressed, gentlemanly-looking man, of apparent even tenor and temper.

This Captain Davis, after his servitude in ropes, tar and tackles, purchased the Rittenhouse estate, at the northwest corner of Arch and Seventh streets, of about sixty feet on Arch street, where the houses of the Messrs. Smith, next above the corner, now stand, and one hundred and twenty feet on Seventh street.

CHAPTER XIV.

THE northeast corner of Race and Water streets was long
and well established, already in 1793, as a mart for the sale
of flour by Thomas Alibone, the grandfather of the late unfortunate President of the Bank of Pennsylvania.

This old gentleman—for so he appeared to me in 1800—
was amongst the most respectable of his calling; and by a
"faithful continuance in well-doing," retired upon the reward
of his integrity and his labors.

Boyer Brooks was his next neighbor and cotemporary, a
boat-builder of notoriety, besides being the author of Brooks's
Court, in Front street above Race.

The dwelling and counting-house of Robert McKean, a
shipping merchant, son of Governor McKean, of 1799, was
as well known next above.

But next above this, there was an old timepiece in the
person and presence of Daniel Thunn, of the firm of Daniel
& Vincent Thunn, merchants, there in 1797 in the German
trade.

Misfortune befell the house; and my venerable friend

Daniel became thereafter clerk to the late Capt. Man, where in the rugged office, over the former's stable on the west side of the yard of the Captain's residence, he calculated interests, commissions and fractions, until he came down in an audible whisper to *"null vom null und nichts,"* i. e. "nothing from nothing, and nothing remains," which became a very current joke of the Captain's whenever he spoke of Mr. Thunn.

He was a very respectable relic of the vicissitudes of mercantile life, and served the Captain for several years, when he retired entirely from the changes and chances of business repousibilities and calculations of interests, to "Rapp's Harmony," where in due time he was gathered to his fathers.

An alley here to Smith's wharf bounded some old stores on Water street and their vacant portions on the wharf, of which an alley above was the northern boundary.

The counting-house of Abraham Piesch presents itself at the upper corner of this alley.

Mr. Piesch was one of the most enterprising shipping merchants of his day, 1800, and onwards. He built more vessels, large and small, than any of his compeers. In the war of 1812 he started twelve schooners on the stocks at the same time, to run the guantlet of blockade or pursuit.

He was largely concerned in the West India trade during the revolution in St. Domingo, and in the East India and European in after time.

He really was a man of mercantile prowess, withal a modest, unassuming, mild-mannered Swiss gentleman. He was shrewd and calculating, but the malignity of war and the cupidity and villany of some of his employees, was more than shrewdness or human foresight could forefend, and he fell a victim to treachery as well as the vast odds of an open and a powerful foe: else, from $100,000 to a $150,000, would have been the balance in his favor even after his failure in 1813–14. But alas! after all his acumen in the various busy projects of mercantile life, he was shrunk by the cold embraces of poverty, and even nudged by the *colder* shoulders of many who had before done him reverence. But such is life!

Jacob Bright's occupancy was divided by an alley to the wharf, on both sides of which were his stores, besides an apartment for large scales for the accommodation of applicants for a knowledge of the weight of their wares.

Bright's wharf and premises were well-known, and their proprietor equally so as a prominent owner of stores, but not a merchant.

A dwelling next above and an alley on the north side to the wharf, brings us to a brewery under the proprietorship and direction of Zachariah Endress.

The most remarkable incumbency of this line was the office of Register of Wills, in charge of George Campbell, where he also resided.

This George Campbell was the father of our late fellow-citizen, George Campbell of Arch street, the third door below Sixth street, north side, who died on the tenth of June, 1855, in his seventy-third year.

The board-yard and counting-house of John Britton cornered this square. It was necessarily of considerable dimensions, and no doubt gave acumen to mensuration, spirit to mechanics, and life to cart wheels, and sometimes bulk to the craft that awaited an export.

VINE TO CALLOWHILL.

Salt, the most invaluable commodity to all animal nature, was here, at the northeast corner of Vine and Water street, in abundance, and Joseph Thomas, West & Jeanes, and Wm. West of the firm of West & Jeanes, were successive operators and very extensive dealers in the article of salt.

The domains were large, and extended northward nearly two hundred feet, divided, however, by an alley to the wharf.

A biscuit bakery, by William Brown, was another popular resort for foreign and domestic supplies. No. 169 heralded the whereabout, and its active proprietor hastened the right hand of fellowship to the patrons of his skill; and now, except the board-yard and counting-house of Stewart & Knight, which also compassed a large lot, there is nothing particular to note to the corner, which was a tavern.

In presenting this view of Water street and the continuation of the mercantile interest of Philadelphia in its scope, I might and could have added much to the catalogue of life that hailed the rising sun and again retired to the hearth as it slept in the west; but, as even now, there were ever and anon inns and outs, which without becoming a succession of Directories, I could not—because it was not my purpose to —follow.

I have endeavored to show who and what represented the commercial interest and influence of our city, within certain limits of time, and I trust have not fallen far short of my purpose; nor could I with such intelligible aid as longevity has afforded from its verdure.

The ancient and very venerable Dr. Collin of the Swedes Church was a reliable chronicle of the olden time; and right happy am I in the experience of elastic, graphic, and comprehensive intellectual memories even in the yellow leaf of human nature; which now, with a very lively picture of the days of my own youth, encourages and impels me to the work and emboldens its truth.   And thus far Water street: but Front street too has its claims, and I shall proceed to show what they were.

CHAPTER XV.

Front street—East side—Callowhill to Vine—Christlieb Bartling—Manuel Eyre—Clawson's tavern—Durham Boats—Joseph Morehane—His School-house.

SEEING that the active elite of life, as well social as mer-cantile, of sixty years ago, was not *confined* to Water street and the wharf, and that important influences—connected more or less with that region, or otherwise of general interest—ranged on the avenue above, I find it but consistent with my project to pass, scan and cull the line of Front street from my original place of beginning, Callowhill street, to my intended terminus, the north side of South street; and although in the review of the limit of this chapter the sources are few, and less fertile than those past and those to come, yet it is not entirely void of interest, if but recalling its original and antique face.

In doing this I may advert to a row of small two and three-story brick houses, of sombre weather-beaten hue even sixty years ago, and tell of a gap here and there between, as air-holes from the river to fan the more condensed atmosphere above; or show the forethought of Father Penn in facilitating ingress and egress to and from Front to Water street by an occasional flight of stone steps. And indeed it will be but a small tribute to the memory of our old friend Christlieb Bartling, to remember him at No. 225, who from that spot in

1802, took his course to some depot of lumber to establish its quality by his inspection, or glance at his stalwart frame as with measured step he made his Sabbath day's journey to and from Dr. Mayer's church, as each returning Sabbath invited him to that sanctuary.

And here too we may see the youthful but manly Manuel Eyre, as his next neighbor, wending his way to his early business associate in furtherance of issues and profits to the firm of Eyre & Massey.

Such were the current possessions of this neighborhood; but there were two other points of marked annals that belong to the history of that compass.

The first was the rear end of a tavern, commencing and fronting principally on Water street, a few doors above Vine street, having the "Rising Sun" for its sign on Water street and the "Constitution and Guerrière" on Front street—it was known as Clawson's tavern, and was the popular resort of the Durham boatmen, who making fast their craft below came up hither to recount their toils in *poling*, or rowing their long-nosed craft through the dangers of shallow streams to the laborious rowing of the deeper waters of the Delaware.

These Durham boats were the usual facilities of conveyance from the flour mills above to the storehouses here below.

They were long and capacious, with prow at both ends, and were steered by a long oar, swung on a pivot at either end, which, however, was more effective on a smooth than a rock-rippled stream, which at the rapids at Trenton defied the skill of the oarsman, and sometimes wrecked his presumption, at the cost of a good load of flour, of which the boats held from one to two hundred barrels.

They derived their name from Durham Creek, Durham Township, Bucks County.

But there was a spot of more personal interest to your author, and though fearful in its nature, was important in effect.

On the very summit of the hill, next or near the corner of Vine street, there was perched an old yellow frame cottage, unfenced of boundary, and free and open to its appurtenances —open to the exuberance of elastic youth—or the arena of study to the more staid and sober host. It was an open common, accessible at all points, and hence the more memorable to wayward youth.

On this spot the lapse moments of scholastic duty found vent in sliding from the top to the bottom of the hill, to the wear and tear of unmentionables, and the total annihilation of our heels.

Joseph Morehane, however, was the *pro tem.* proprietor of the domain, and the centre of gravity in the cot on the summit.

Here the schoolmaster was seldom abroad, but on the contrary, his tenacious presence, with his flexible rattan, was a rod of *terrorem* to undisciplined youth, and the active evidence that to spare the rod would be to spoil the child, *his* forbearance truly was great; but the memento before us sometimes trespassed upon *ours.*

These were the days of hobgoblins, ghosts and witches, of which some of the elder boys took advantage to test the powers of their master and his old lady, by an inverted horseshoe over the door to check their egress; but, alas for the prank, the penalty of the rattan was the hasty successor to the sport.

Although our master was scarcely threescore years of age, extreme youth thought of nothing but extreme age in him; the battery of his mouth was gone, and the jaws cringed for a substitute. Moreover, being small in stature, and sparse of flesh, he appeared to shrink in the cold embrace of old time.

I have been informed by those who knew him better than I could have done, that he was a well educated man—a *literati*—a man of good character; and in the latter part of his life, employed as book-keeper to Samuel Lehman, of the Northern Liberties, ship-smith.

Mr. Morchane lived to the good old age of eighty-eight years, and died on the 19th of December, 1831.

CHAPTER XVI.

Front street, West side—Callowhill to Vine—A Black Bear Tavern—Isaac W. Norris—Isaiah Jeanes—Capt. James King—Joseph Copperthwaite—"Bully White"—Daniel Bacon—William West—Fitch's Steamboat, 1788.

THE west side of this square was lined with a better class of houses, and several of our more prominent citizens were resident there.

It was, however, not without its mixture of small tenements, and they appropriated to divers uses of stores, groceries, and amongst others, a distillery and a tavern.

This tavern was known by its sign of a Black Bear, and was situated about one third of the way south of the corner of Callowhill, occupying some forty feet front, having a wide opening at its side, as an entrance to the grounds in the rear for the accommodations pertinent to the entertainment of man and horse.

Isaac W. Norris, once a supercago, afterward, 1811, a shipchandler at the southeast corner of Water and Vine streets, occupied one of the best three-story brick houses, about midway of the row.

Mr. Norris was a remarkably fine-looking, well-built and handsome man, and as gentle, in proportion, to all intents and purposes; a very pleasurable review of my own personal business transactions with him in my onset in business life.

He died January 5th, 1847, aged sixty-two years.

The root, Isaiah, of the present family of Jeanes's, salt merchants, at one time in connection with the West's; and some of the branches were resident, in 1805, at No. 196, and in 1811, more in detail perhaps, at No. 208.

The place that knew the old-time fixture, Captain James King, but now knows him no more, was No. 210, a first-class three-story brick, with porch and portico, wherein the Captain was resident for many years.

He was crippled by the loss of his foot, occasioned by a throw from his carriage, and which confined his locomotion to a wheel-chair, in which he passed himself from spot to spot as call required.

His competency, however, mitigated in some degree his misfortune, and spared him the pain or inconvenience of thought for the morrow—that was already guarded.

Capt. King was the half-brother of our late citizen, Joseph Worrel, whose mother, commonly called "Nanny King," was as well the mother of Mr. Worrel.*

Near by Captain King, at No. 204, was the seat of justice and terror to evil doers, where Joseph Copperthwaite administered the law, and by testimony imposed the penalty or discharged the accused, 1802.   Prior to this, Mr. Copperthwaite under the authority of High Sheriff vested in him, dealt out the wrath of the law against delinquent debtors and, perhaps, candidates for more stringent measures.

He was High Sheriff, and had to perform the duties—profit-

---

* Nanny King was a lively and anecdotal relic of Revolutionary times. She was a woman of high spirit, of plain and very honest bearing. She lived by herself, under the care of the Captain, at the head of Goddard's alley, in Second street, running eastward, a little above Vine, 1798, 1800, and onward, to her final exit.

able, disagreeable, or repulsive—of that office. All this sixty years ago.

There was, however, at No. 193, perhaps the most notorious individual of our community at that time, long before, and even long after 1800.

Capt. William White, generally known as "Bully White," was of Revolutionary date, even in old age a steady old salt, of iron frame and feature, worn stern by practical necessities; said to have commanded a privateer in the Revolution, and subsequently a playfellow with the froth of Neptune.

This well-built, heavy, round-shouldered, notorious mariner, with heavy, jutting gray eyebrows, and slow but characteristic step, made his daily sortie from the house of Captain Joseph Vansise, from No. 193, where and whence he was as well known as any man in Philadelphia; commanding respect for his person, his indomitable courage, and his general history.

His countenance, at rest, was by no means savage, but rather kindly.

I have often seen him, but never with any repulsive feeling. His calling, its duties, and his judgment, made him a disciplinarian and a commander to be respected; but if Captain or "Bully White" was any thing but a liberal and—worldly called—good-hearted man, his contour belied him.

He owned and commanded a brig, called the "Betsy," noted as a fast sailer. Captain White was patronized, socially and commercially, by Harvey & Davis, of Race and Water streets, ship-chandlers.

It would be a slight to pass a tradesman of as much importance to the piscatory sportsman, as was friend Daniel Bacon, who, a few doors above the corner of Vine, made his calling known by a well-represented shad, or something like

7

it, suspended by hook and line, over his door here. Here, fiishing-tackle, to all intents and purposes, was to be found; and here too, in the early part of this century, was the resort of connoisseurs and adepts in the art of catching fish.

William West, the pioneer in the salt trade, cornered the row with a mansion of dignified appearance; whence, from the ease and comforts of his family hearth, he could oversee his business quarters at the corner below, and be at the command of any emergency.

The width of the street, east of Front, here gave the north-west corner of Front and Vine the advantage of an unobstructed view of the wharf and the Delaware.

It was opposite to this opening off Vine-street wharf, in the middle of the stream, in the year 1788, that John Fitch's steamboat—the first discovery of that mode of applying steam—made her *debut*, with her crude machinery, in her first trip to Burlington, N. J., passing over the tide at the rate of three miles an hour, to the great joy of the multitude on the wharf witnessing the feat. Her paddles were in the shape of large oars, when in an upright position, broad at the top and tapering downward; and when set in motion, created a furor of huzzas.

The presence and eye-witness of my friend, Mr. Charles Massey, at this exhibition, is a good voucher for this fact, who further informs me that Fitch was assisted in his scheme by Lewis Braill, of Brewer's alley, a blacksmith, who made the boiler and other apparatus to complete the machinery, aided by Henry Voigt, a watchmaker, in Second above Race; they were both men of great mechanical genius.

This embryo of steamboat navigation, was a birth of tribu lation, patience, and expense, of which the real parent, after thus laying the track for the prosperity of the million, himself died poor, neglected, unwept.

It is said that Fitch caught the idea from a tea-kettle, in the spout of which he had fixed a cork—perhaps to hasten his supper by confining the steam—but the increasing force of the vapor displaced it; and the forceful " pop !" gave force to thought—thought to ingenuity and the trophy to perseverance.

CHAPTER XVII.

Front street, East side—Vine to Race—Isaac Jones—Abraham Piesch—John
Wharton—William Fling, Senior and Junior—Peter Brown—Praise Woodman.

FROM this corner, down to the steps, an avenue to Water
street, about midway of the square, there is nothing particular
to note. The houses, already in 1800, were old, weather-
beaten and frost-bitten; the basement being a very available
entrance, covered by an almost perpendicular cellar-door, ad-
mitting a full-sized person, without bend or nod, to the apartment under the first floor.

Isaac Jones, however, is not to be passed in silence; for at
the south corner of the steps above alluded to, his snuff and
tobacco emporium was as well known as himself as proprietor, and the old gentleman was not unmindful of his importance. His profession was available, for snuff, tobacco and
cigars were desirable luxuries even of that day.

The humble and unpretending Abraham Piesch was his
next door neighbor, resident there, and occupying through to
Water street, the lower story being the depot of his imports;
where the hills and hollows of coffee-bags were enviable in-
vitations to his "cubs" to play hide-and-seek, to which your
humble servant was a gladsome party.

As my early friend, Mr. Piesch, has gone down to the
valley of oblivion, unwept and unsung by his mercantile asso-

ciates, I cannot pass him here without again referring to his character and standing, as a man of wealth and prosperity to the turn of his tide, yet a man of humble bearing, of equable deportment without reference to grades, with a currency of benevolence passing him very acceptably through his various relations in life, as a very mild, soft-spoken, untempered gentleman.

And here I take temporary leave of Abraham Piesch, and introduce my reader to

John Wharton, of No. 165, next door below; this gentleman—as denominated in those days—was a surgeon-barber, and heralded by a tin sign on his window-shutter, representing a female figure seated in sickly attitude, with outstretched arm, either awaiting the click of the lancet, or shying at the crimson spurt into the bowl held by the thoughtful Sangrado.

Mr. Wharton was a man of character, and the determination of his countenance, sharpened by an oblique cast of his eye, were unmistakable warnings that he was not to be trifled with.

A few doors below, at No. 155, in a two-story brick house,* a little back from the line, having a pale-fence in front, and gate of entrance, dwelt a popular house painter and glazier of his day.

William Fling seemed to be the chosen to paint and beautify the steeple of Christ Church, and all belonging to it. And often have I seen him, and his son who succeeded him, or some of their employees, pendent from the spire, two hundred feet in mid-air, in a deep basket, plying the brush with perfect nonchalance, to the admiration of some and the fear

---

* This house is still standing, under new No. 223, occupied as a cooper-shop, enclosed by a high, board fence.

and terror of others of the many lookers-on below; but I never heard of an accident from that source.

William Fling, Jr., was, in stature and general appearance, a *fac simile* of his senior, both men of courage, for in that day it was a feat to venture two hundred feet above the heads below. And whether they, or either of them, trusted to the " Yo, heave ho !" below, or sent up a maintop-sail man as a substitute, they endorsed the project, and were responsible for results.

Peter Brown's blacksmith shop occupied a space a little below, No. 141; it was a frame, and run through to Water street.

Praise Woodman must have been notorious for name, if even nature, education, or occupation beclouded the popularity due to his, or her existence, for I do not know how to *sex* that surname. Suffice it to say, that, in 1795, Praise Woodman kept a boarding-house at the northeast corner of Race and Front streets, and thus cornered the row now reviewed.

The row, from Jones's down to the corner, escaped the conflagration of 1850, leaving even yet a good sample of the olden time.

CHAPTER XVIII.

DESULTORY as may have been some of the marks and
remarks in the line of march along Front street, thus
far, that now before us has even more *point d'appui* for
the life, natural, scientific, and historical, of sixty years
ago.

In many neighborhoods there are certain *nuclei*, stereotyp-
ing their identity by successive generations; their grand-
fathers were born, reared, and educated there, and progeny
claims antiquity to the spot of their sires.

Thus the Stackhouses and the Starrs, particularly the
former, who date even from 1793, were amongst the earliest
residents of that quarter, and types of their generations to this
day, they contributed their share to the prominent variety,
and enlivened the busy scenes of mercantile and mechanical
industry; for whilst Amos Stackhouse beat the "Cooper's
march" at No. 168, John Starr retired daily from the labors
of selling flour and salt to No. 152. They were respectable
tenants there, and a part of its active life.

But there was more than ordinary interest in this compass.

The prow of the dignified merchantmen awaited its embellish-
ment here, and the skill of an eminent sculptor became the
pride of a shipowner.

Mr. William Rush was a carver of distinction, and without
a rival in the United States or Europe.

The figure-heads of most all of our merchant ships were the
work of his hand, and generally admitted to be good likenesses
of their originals. His "William Penn," "General Washington," "Franklin," "Voltaire," "Rousseau," and "General
Wade Hampton," with many others, were amongst the
prominent specimens of his art.

They were full-length, life-like, full-dressed figures, the
Generals in regimentals, and the others in plain garb.

The representation of the Crucifixion, in St. Augustine's
Church, was the boast of the city, for the accuracy of its delineations at the hands of William Rush.

Time, in due course, scathed the features, and the frag-
ments of the former; after they had served their day and
generation—but alas, for a reckless mob—the torch of the
incendiary of 1844, fired by an unholy, unrighteous, and in-
human spirit of persecution, destroyed the temple, the altar,
and its adornments at one fell swoop.

This piece of sculpture was of life size, and generally con-
sidered his *chef d'œuvre*.

But, thanks to the careful leading of some of our former
city Fathers, who protected and preserved the life-sized
female figure with her spouting swan, that once ornamented
the Centre Square, where, as a fountain, from a rather
careless heap of rocks, in front of the white marble building, she stood alone, and was the admiration of the daily
throng.

This figure now perpetuates the memory of its skillful

sculptor, on a ledge in a nook of Fairmount, where, whilst it contributes to the beautiful blending of art with nature, she spreads the fame of Rush in rainbow tints, fed and impelled from the crystal fountain at her feet.

The studio of Mr. Rush was a two-story frame, numbered 172, a few doors above Key's alley. There was a large log under his front windows, from which, we little boys, on our way to, and from school, peeped and wondered at the transformation of unwrought timber to the form and appearance of a human being.

Mr. Rush was rather below medium height, well formed, genteel appearance, and very intelligent countenance.

He died at the age of seventy-six, on the 17th January, 1833.

Let it not be the step from the sublime to the ridiculous, to come down from the arts and sciences, to "kiss a cup, and pass it to the rest"—and yet a good cup of tea is not to be despised.

A very popular emporium for this luxury was at No. 168, where Rebecca Inkson, 1795, and long after, dealt out the material for the social beverage, and was patronized to her own comforts by the very *vox populi*, as well for her assortment of teas as for her appendages of dry goods and trimmings.

A mixture is not complete without ingredients, and therefore permit me to notice our old friend, Jacob Wayne, cabinet and chair-maker, of No. 166, and the famous spinning-wheel, that insignia'd the occupation, in front and over the door of John B. Ackley, at the corner of Fearis's court, the first inlet below Key's alley, No. 150, in 1802.

There was a passage through here to Second street, principally for the accommodation of Friends to their meeting-house in Key's alley.

This same John B. Ackley was afterward druggist and apothecary, and sold paints, at the west end of this avenue.

Solomon Park was a fixture in this neighborhood, from and before 1791, in which, within a small compass, he was variously located, but my personal data finds, and knows him at No. 146, in 1800.

Here, in a gray, weather-beaten, old-fashioned three-story brick, was the watch-making, mending and repairing establishment of Solomon Park.

The front entrance was high above the pavement, and could only be reached by a high flight of steps, beside which an almost perpendicular cellar-door—apparently leaning against the wall—closed the entrance to the basement or cellar.

From this spot emerged, from day to day, the tall, gaunt figure of Solomon Park; his movement was pendulum-like, and apparently in time with its clock. He was, to all intents and purposes, an old time-piece, in keep with the rack and racket of his elliptic bulk-window and its old-fashioned contents.

Although a model of primitive simplicity in apparel, there was sportive fancy in the man, for he had the reputation of being a "Nimrod" in the chase, and kept a "rosinant" to further his fancy, which, with his master, grew gray in the service of his fanciful pastime.

Variety does not cease here—a barber-shop belongs to the range, and due respect must be allotted to George Vanderslice, the proprietor, especially as Mr. Vanderslice was not a thing of a day, but flourished in his trade here, and carried his occupation to Race above Third street, where for many years after he was the popular tonsure of the day.

He was a good Methodist, and stood well in the community.

The house next below the corner of Coates's alley, was a mansion of some dignity, having a front of about thirty feet, and proportioned in height; it was the largest house in that square; it stands a little oblique from the proper line, arising probably from its erection before the proper grade was laid down.

It was built, 1764,* by William Rush, black and ship-smith, the father-in-law of its occupant, Robert Bethel, in 1791, who lived there for many years. Mr. Bethel, the grandparent of our present Robert Bethel, Esq., was a ship-chandler on Bickley's wharf, by profession—a highly respectable old gentleman, and socially in keeping with his character and standing.

In connection with his wife's family, the venerable General Irvine was a fireside companion.

This old gentleman was an associate of General Washington, having served under him in the American Revolution.

He was a pink of neatness, whose black suit, short-clothes, and silver-buckled shoes and old-fashioned cocked-hat, rendered him in appearance more of a civilian, or even a D.D., than a tactician in fire-arms.

If, however, his respectability had been measured by his size, he would have lost in degrees. But not so; his character

---

* This mansion is now in the occupancy of Peter Maisson, whose extensive biscuit bakery is next door above, on the corner of Coates's alley.

Mr. Bethel died in Holmesburg, April 17, 1852, in the seventy-sixth year of his age.

and bearing gave tone to his *position*, making his mark upon some one to memorialize his existence.

He was, as hinted above, of medium height, light built, very neat in apparel, very measured in his gait, and had more the appearance of a Divine than a brandisher of sword and shield.

General James Irvine is entitled to the following further notice.

First. He occupied the mansion above-mentioned from the close of the Revolution to the year 1819.

Second. Although a hatter by trade, in early life he became a soldier of two wars, being engaged in 1764 on the frontier of our State in Indian warfare; and again in the American Revolution, under General Washington, losing three fingers of his right hand on the plains of Germantown.

He served after the war in several of the Councils of the State, and died in 1819, an aged veteran of time and labor, full of the honors due to the merits of his life and character.

His house (above) became, by will I presume, the property of Mrs. Francis Irvine Brown, daughter of *Captain* Robert Bethel—for before he settled down in a ship-chandlery, he *was* a sea-captain—and was a near kinsman of my venerable cocked-hat, General James Irvine.

In passing on to the corner of Race street, it is but civil to notice Mrs. Hannah Marshall, whose boarding-house cornered Brooks's court. She was well-known there in 1802, and was succeeded by her daughter Bathsheba—known as Bashy Marshall—who continued there for many years after, but—

In 1799, the firm of Ducoing & Lacombe had their counting-house at this corner; they were in the Bordeaux and West India trade, large importers of wines, brandies and silks; their counting-house was afterward removed into

Coates's alley near Front, where in 1802, our present fellow-citizen, Mr. J. P. Fontanges, served them as clerk for several years.

Mr. Fontanges was afterward of the firm of Chapron, Frenaye & Co., in the silk and ribbon business, at the north-west corner of Seventh and Market streets.

He is now a retired merchant and has his office in Gold street, south side of the bank of Pennsylvania.

The corner of Race and Front was a bunch of old red frames, the edge of which, east and west, was occupied for many years as a cabinet-maker shop by William Rigby, whose popularity was coequal with the rest of his fortunes.

In connection with this square, it may be proper to note that it had four insertions from Vine street: first, Fearis's court; second McCullough's court; third, Coates's alley; and fourth, Brooks's court. Of these, though our subsequently opulent citizen, John Stille, Jr., occupied a rather imposing three-story brick house, with pediment front, at the head of McCullough's court, Brooks's court was by no means least in importance.

Bowyer Brooks, Sen. & Jun., boat-builders, were men of business on the wharf—but resident there; but there was one of more public notoriety, of an entirely different character, adding to the respectability of this nook.

Rebecca Jones was an acceptable preacher of the Society of Friends, highly esteemed for her consistency of character and spiritual dealings in their meetings, and there and then, some sixty years ago, was a profitable example to that circle. She died in 1817, in the seventy-eighth year of her age.

Rosanna Donnel too, a good, old Roman Catholic, kept her faith there, and behaved accordingly; and her daughter,

Mary Donnel, her worthy successor in faith and practice, contributed their mite to the favor of good things to come.

Antipodes as they were in profession, they were one in pursuit, and qualified the atmosphere (that else might have edged the source of respiration,) with the smoother zephyrs of " love to thy neighbor."

CHAPTER XIX.

A BISCUIT BAKERY has been a fixture on this line from time immemorial: for already in 1791, No. 127, near the corner, was a popular resort for biscuits, large or small, wholesale and perhaps retail.

Frederick Christian was an early proprietor, of 1791, here; was succeeded by his son Peter—afterward Alderman Christian—and now and for some years past is far-famed as Watson's more extensive biscuit bakery.

John Keffer, however, was well-known as a thrifty, industrious, and attentive shoemaker at No. 123, in 1793. In those days little boys wore what were familiarly known as "Kaks,"* a rather fanciful fit to our tiny feet, and Mr. Keffer made them.

A little below this a blank wall protected the culinary department, and very small yard in front of it, of No. 119, a

---

* "Kaks" were shoes for small boys, embellished with a yellow streak called "rand," inserted between the sole and the seam of the upper. Which, proud as we were to get them on, were even more so in due time to get them off, being beneath notice whilst in "Kaks."

venerable pile of earlier date, wide front, spacious and re-spectable.

It was the habitation of Pattison Hartshorne, of the firm of Hartshorne, Large & Co., dry goods merchants, 1793.

Again, a little below, two other very imposing three-story mansions claimed respect. Of these, No. 107 was the residence of J. H. C. Heineken, agent of the Bavarian Republic, 1807; the other, No. 105, was in the occupancy of Simon Probasco, a Notary Public, a terror to the unmindful of bank hours and their three o'clock requirements: for doubtless, "protests" were scaled at, and delivered from No. 105 North Front street.

A flight of steps here to Water street intercepts the course, and a wall on their south side, protective of a chasm behind it, leads to the printing-office of the famous Richard Folwell.

Dickey Folwell—for such was his cognomen—was the racy editor of the "Spirit of the Press," a small, but characteristic sheet, redolent of wit, humor and sarcasm, and unsparing of its subjects.

Dickey was an indomitable wit, and whether "four fingers and a thumb" knocked him down for it, or the hilarity of his gaysome chums lit up his convivialities, it was the same to him. Wit or sarcasm, or revenge in that form, was in him, and must and did come out.

He was full of talent, but it got into a wrong channel. Moreover, Temperance societies were in *futuro*, and Dickey was innocent of their meaning. His editorial issues, therefore, were subjects of unchastened wit and often very unrefined report; and woe to the wight that even showed slight upon Dickey Folwell.

His paper was the nucleus of all its like in after time. He was small of stature, indifferent to apparel, wore spectacles, often minus one glass, and by no means chaste in his witticisms.

Passing a boarding-house, and the shoemaker shop of Richard Miles of No. 72, we come to a nest of frames of two stories, inhabited and appropriated as follows:

The first was occupied by Jacob Martin as residence and chair manufactory. Mr. Martin was a tall man, of medium locomotion—the reverse of his son Abraham Martin, the active and efficient officer of the Sunday School Union, who must have inherited his energies from his mother, which, with the steadiness of his father, with uncompromising principles of his own, makes him what he certainly is, a valuable member of the community.

Nathaniel Bayne was next neighbor here, a dapper little man, active, industrious and speedy. He was a turner, and turned out tops of all sorts and sizes for the amusement of boys in top season. He and his wife were a happy pair in form and social feature; they had no children; were good neighbors, and enjoyed the respect of all about them.

Mr. Bayne died on the 20th of April, 1847, in his eighty-fifth year; but Mrs. Bayne is yet living, and now an inmate of the "Widow's Asylum" of Eighteenth and Cherry street.

William Bowen was another specimen of the olden time, next below. A steady handicraftsman, and well skilled in the art of chair-making. These three last all date from before 1791, as fixtures there.

Isaac Wainwright bounds these frames by a very respectable three-story brick; it was of modern appearance and character in 1800, and from the steps down the best and handsomest house. Mr. Wainwright was a respectable member of the Society of Friends; a good citizen and estimable neighbor.

8

A blue two-storied frame here varied the scene, and our old friend and neighbor, Melchoir Wisinger, helped the variety by the general flow of his wit, humor and friendly familiarity with young folks.

He was a wire-worker by trade, vented his genius in the back room of his lower story, and exhibited its fruits in bird-cages, sieves, etc., at the front window and door, where a review shows up the old gentleman in his porch, resting and supporting one of his legs—unbent and unbending from a white-swelling in his youth—fondling and joking with the youth of the neighborhood as they came within his call.

His dame—second wife—erewhile the "Widow Sykes," is entitled to a tribute. She was handmaid to industry and frugality, and economized even day-dawn to lengthen time. She and Peter Hahn's boy were competitors for the first ray, of whom it was quaintly said that they both staid up all night for the prize in the morning.

This old lady died April 26th, 1851, in her ninetieth year.

She had had her day of fascination, and admiration followed her to the porch of her second matrimonial embark, for a jilted "Cœlebs" often sat himself in an opposite porch, solilo-quizing his mishap, and denouncing her liege lord as an im-perfect concern.

This is a sample of the olden time. Human nature echoes "*Idem.*"

Peter Delamar was a nautical instrument-maker next below, in the house afterward the residence of Singleton, the son-in-law of Mrs. Holland, of Front near Market, of whom more anon.

Beer-houses were less obnoxious than under our present code of refinement. A pint of beer was an allowable beverage, and a room for its enjoyment was undisputed authority for its legality. A good Presbyterian could and did vend and measure the juice of malt, with its hop tonic, *sans reproche*, without fear of censure from Session or Presbytery.

Joseph Brittin was the exemplary *maitre d'hote* here, highly esteemed, well-mannered, and a proper disciplinarian of his domestic circle; neither broils nor enemies grew upon his soil, nor aught of evil to disparage his claims to good citizenship.

Odds and ends in society have been and ever will be.

The corner was without notoriety, except that it was a boarding-house, kept by Mrs. Phœbe Wady; but there was spice of a peculiar nature in it.

John Scurlog was a bachelor, and a Roman Catholic decidedly opposed to Protestantism in any form. He was wont to amuse, and perhaps vent himself from his door-step on Sundays, and soliloquize ridicule upon church-goers thus:—

"Look at that auld divil! She's going to meetin', and the divil a word will she hear or say." Again, "There goes another. He's going to church to say 'we've done those things that we oughtn't to have done,' and as soon as he gets out, he'll do it over again;" and thus he would conclude— "One divil jumps out of another." He was, however, an innocent odd one.

CHAPTER XX.

THE southwest corner of Race and Front streets was occupied in 1802, by Charles Cavender, as his grocery store and
residence, who was at the same time a local preacher of the
Methodist church.

Dr. George F. Alberti was resident next below, at No. 116,
in 1805.

This house was an ancient structure of brick, three stories
in height, but about sixteen feet in front; elevation to the
first floor, some five or six steps.

In the front room—a very small one—he had his epitome
of an apothecary shop, where he compounded his curatives
preparatory to his professional visits, always carrying his
medical intentions in the side pocket of his coat.

The Doctor was a dapper little gentleman, of independent
but very thoughtful carriage, fraught with wit, humor, and
Esculapean wisdom, tossing his queue in keeping with the up
and down of his heart. He was a man of kindly tempera-

ment and great suavity of manner; but an expletive would sometimes muddle the stream of his amiability, and dash the modesty of an erring patient.

His usual mode of addressing his *female* patients was, "Honey," "My dear," in soft, musical tones.

On a visit to a lady, his softest and most sympathetic inquiry was, "Well, my dear, how are you this morning?"

"Why, Doctor, I'm not very well—not as well as yesterday."

"The silent Doctor shook his head," and his queue instanter popped up from the collar of his coat as he dropped his chin upon his breast.

"Ahem!" said he. "Why, honey, what's the matter? I left you comfortable yesterday. Where, my dear, is your pain?"

(This was not an amorous expression of affection, for his patient was his senior.)

"Oh! my Doctor," she replied, "in the pit of my stomach!" Again the queue wagged the motion of his thoughts.

"Sorry to hear it, my dear," said he, sympathetically; "pray what have you been eating?"

"Why nothing, Doctor, but a few *new potatoes*." Down went the queue as up went the head.

"New potatoes!" exclaimed he. "New potatoes! The devil you have. Why, what the devil did you do that for, madam?"

"Why, Doctor!——"

"Why, the devil," said he, "no wonder at your pain in the pit of the stomach! New potatoes," murmured he—"the devil;" but the antidote was in his side pocket, and a nauseous dose was the penalty.

The Doctor thought well of his companionship with Dr.

Physic, as student, and had claims to his skill as M.D. in after life.

He was a fond patron of matrimony, having himself pledged his troth some two or three times at the altar of Hymen.

He passed time's ordeal until the 22d of June, 1837, enrolled him in the catalogue of the past, and gathered him to his fathers, in the seventy-second year of his age.

In 1795, Abraham Kintzing occupied No. 114, next below Dr. Alberti's.

This gentleman was of the firm of Pratt & Kintzing; in appearance very respectable, dignified, and gentlemanly; in reputation, a merchant of the first order; in character, shrewd and attentive; and untiring in the pursuits of his firm, of which he had the credit of being *the* merchant.

He was of medium stature, and steady, thoughtful movement.

In 1796, Henry Pratt bought the mansion of Isaac Wharton, the father of the late Thomas I. Wharton, Esq., remodeled, modernized, and freshened it to distinction above its neighbors, so that No. 112 knew not its former state. Here Mr. Pratt took up his abode, from his former residence in Water street.*

It was a rather depressed three-story brick, but about forty feet in front, with broad and high marble steps to its entrance, which was in the centre, having parlors, with two full-sized windows each, on either side of the hall or entry.

---

* Immediately after Mr. H. Pratt's removal from Water street, Peter Care, an eminent miller and flour merchant, took possession of the homestead, and pursued his dealings in flour at that point.

Mr. Care was the *last* father-in-law of Mr. Pratt, as allied to Miss Susan Care, she being his third wife.

It stood some ten or twelve feet back from the line, which gave it lawn and railing, beautifying as protecting the domain within; in addition to this, a carriage-way on the south side, helped the guarantee of its character and title to respect.

Henry Pratt was a son of Matthew Pratt, an eminent limner of 1758, connected in history with our late Dr. Philip Syng Physic, whose grandfather, Philip Syng, Sr., being a goldsmith, tutored the father of our Matthew Pratt, in that art.

The works of Matthew Pratt are still extant in the Pratt family, and have borne the test of contrast and criticism with the most eminent artists; for a more extensive account, see Dunlap's history of the "Rise and Progress of the Arts and Design in the United States," vol. 1, p. 98.

Thomas Pratt was also a scion of the above stem, and had his day at No. 52 South Wharves, as a respectable shipping merchant, in 1805.

Henry Pratt died on the 6th of February, 1837, in his seventy-seventh year, leaving his brother, Thomas Pratt, the survivor of the parentage.

He is yet, though eighty-six years of age, in the full enjoyment of life; and being of sound mind, memory and understanding, is a very intelligent and companionable old gentleman.

In this immediate neighborhood, and between 112 and the corner, there was a wine-bottling cellar, kept by a long, tall, gaunt Frenchman, whose daily companion seemed to be a tutored cat, tamed, domesticated, and familiarized; and so far the boon companion of her master, that she might be seen frequently at his side, or near him, taking cellar-doors, steps and the wall, for her instinctive protection from dogs.

No. 110 was a large three-story brick mansion of full forty feet in front, door in the centre, parlors each side of the hall, elevation considerable, surmounted by a high flight of gray-stone steps, wide and easy.

This was the residence of Henry Drinker, a valuable member of the Society of Friends, a kind-hearted, benevolent gentleman—*sans* boots, spurs or lapels—a "friend in need," as I am happy in the opportunity to show.

An ancient friend of mine had sold one property to buy another; but his purchaser, jealous of the transaction, withheld the consideration in order to supplant him in the operation. *Nonplussed* by the suspension, he went to a lawyer who had professed friendship and proffered services in any future emergency, to whom he essayed to state his case; but, this limb of the law, forgetting his friendly invitation, paced his office floor to and fro, whistling the appeal into *vacuum;* finally, however, he stopped short and said, "Jacob, don't thee know, *no pay, no pater noster?*"

In this dilemma—for he was poor, and had no pay for *this* "pater noster"—he went to his friendly neighbor, about a square off, and stated his difficulty and danger of losing his bargain.

Mr. Drinker heard his complaint, and impromptu thus responded:

"Jacob, go at once and procure writings to confirm thy purchase, and I'll lend thee the money, (£100,) till thee gets thine." And this he did without fee, reward or security, 1793.

Such was Henry Drinker, of 110 North Front street; and as far as I have known the Drinker family since, they did not fall far from that tree, for they were a goodly folk.

Drinker's alley takes this family name, for it runs on the south side of these premises through to Second street.

The southwest corner of this alley was occupied, in 1795, as a tallow-chandlery, by Archibald Gardner, but subsequently by Richard Wall, 1807, and many years after as a Windsor chair manufactory.

Already in 1796, there was a very venerable pair at No. 104.

Christian Hahn was a prominent manufacturer of chocolate and mustard. His manufactory was on the rear of his lot, and the chocolate-nuts ground, melted, mixed and moulded there.

The grinding was done by horse-power. I have often seen the poor beast tread the circle round and round again, without coming to any point, until 11 o'clock A. M. gave respite to him and his masters.

The welcome "punch-bowl" in turn awaited release of *its* burthen—for a refreshment of some kind was customary at about 11 o'clock, in that day—our workmen therefore hastened to the agreeable emolient to their dusted throats, where, under good cheer, they quaffed their portion, and crushed their bread and cheese.

This respectable couple were original members—from the German Lutheran—of Dr. Mayer's English Lutheran church, and it fell to my lot to escort the old lady to the old Academy in Fourth street, to hear his first sermon.

Mrs. Hahn was a small body, whilst Dr. Mayer was of full stature; but, returning from the service, the old lady said, that he was a "fine *little man*."

I am happy to salt her memory, as a very fine, good, little woman; and her husband, as a good, peace-loving citizen.

Ephraim Haines was a merchant of another sort; but his

extensive dealings in mahogany, made him widely known, and at home at No. 100.

He afterward purchased the lot and frame of the eminent carver, Rush, No. 172, and built himself a residence on that artistic spot—a spot sacred to the memory of art and science in the United States.

At No. 98, a bag punctured with feathers showed forth the calling of Henry Slesman, as a dealer in that article.

Mr. Slesman was a quiet neighbor in practice as well as by nature, for from some remote cause he had lost the edge of his voice and he spoke softly.

He lived here for many years after 1795.

John Skyren—noted in the diagram—was resident at the upper corner of Elfrith's alley, No. 96 in 1805.

Sharon Carter, noted page 30, was resident at the south corner of Elfrith's alley, No. 94 in 1802.

In this compass, a little below the above corner, an old tenement with almost erect cellar-door, exhibiting at its opening onions, sausages, potatoes, fish, and a variety of edibles with their various odors, was the general whereabouts of a certain darkey, called "Joe," a one-string musician or banjoist, which with his thumb, the only facility of his right hand, he tickled day in and day out, to the amusement of the boys and the arrest of a penny from more mature admirers. Joe was an original on the banjo, and gave tone to his immediate atmosphere, unobstructed in vibration on my ear even to the present time.

John Webb, a very excellent member of the Society of Friends, occupied No. 88. He was a cabinet-maker by trade, and had his shop in the rear.

The grading of the street here left the original ground-floor or parlor one story above its earlier location, and made the late cellar a tenantable basement.

Mr. Webb was a practically pious man, keeping his end in view by the *memento mori* of his own measured coffin under his bed. He was a preacher of the Society of Friends.

The basement above alluded to was tenanted by a certain Catharine Hanningrout, commonly known as "Old Katy," who sold apples, cakes, candies, and small beer in the front part, and had her *boudoir* in a floorless department in the rear. "Katy" had been evidently a fine-looking woman in her younger day; but alas! for the ruthless ravages of time, she was even bowing to its mandate already in my earliest day: for eighty years were even then her portion.

Length of days and decency of apparel ascribed wealth to her reputation, which a youth of twenty-four eyeing with eager covetousness, crawled to her blind side, captured her, and decoyed her to a matrimonial alliance.

Poor "Old Katy!" the penalty of her folly was the annihilation of her domestic comforts.

In 1802 a burly baker, Henry Dankel, with more than the ordinary allotment of flesh and blood, was master of a bakery in the old two-story brick house next below; who was succeeded by Godfrey Seveke in 1807, and who, like his predecessor, throve and grew fat by the daily issues of twist and hot rolls in the morning, and the savory roasts at noon. This was a sustentation fund of the neighborhood.

The row here was broken by an inlet for egress from, and ingress to stables and other conveniences in the rear.

The south side of this alley was bounded by the chair-manufactory of Gilbert Gaw, there already in 1795, and long after, indeed until death itself smothered his existence in the conflagration of his premises.

Mr. Gaw was a good citizen though a severe disciplinarian; but his efforts for obedience were as striking out, as in-doors, seeing that a street-brawl would bring him with almost constabulary authority to the rescue of peace and good order.

Melchoir Larer took state next below, as brewer and bottler of *malt liquor*—VASTLY DIFFERENT FROM ITS ABOMINABLE APOLOGY UNDER THE NAME OF LAGER-BEER, A PERNICIOUS AND DECEITFUL DECOY TO THE BAR AND THE BOTTLE, A SWILL, MORE TO THE DESTRUCTION OF THE BODY AND SOUL OF MAN THAN RUM OR ANY OF ITS AFFINITIES IN GROG SHOP, TAVERN, OR HOTEL.

The Trenton stage-office swung its sign over the pavement of No. 82, where the crack of the whip of the waiting driver often enlivened the early morn as a call to those within and a show to those without.

The house was old and rusty (brick), had very high steps to the bar-room, and was kept by John Carpenter (1802), a man of extra size, contrasting extensively with his minimum better-half—literally half—for she could easily pass under his outstretched arm.

John Inskeep, from the same occupation at No. 46 Arch street, under the sign of the "Jolly Bacchus" in 1793, was Alderman Inskeep at No. 80 North Front street, next below the stage-office, 1802.

Here an arched alley broke the line; this alley was the entrance to the stables of James C. Fisher, who occupied the mansion in front on Arch street, and the stores of Samuel Allen, whose counting-house and dwelling was a few doors above Mr. Fisher.

The south corner of the alley was the residence of Alexander James Dallas, the father of our cotemporary George M. Dallas, Minister-Plenipotentiary, etc., etc.

Mr. Dallas was then, 1795, Secretary of the Commonwealth of Pennsylvania.

He was a remarkable fine-looking man, full size, well built, and well-dressed; a very prominent part of his apparel was a brown coat, and his finish a well-powdered head, with clubbed hair rolling a circle of powder on and below the collar of his coat.

Mr. Dallas was an eminent jurist and constituted no small part of the dignity of our upper Courts, where I have often seen him, when at leisure, sitting with his right hand resting in the bosom of his half-buttoned coat, to the admiration of more than your author.

We are here on the ground of the old Quaker Bank Meeting House, which was considerably elevated, and whither Friends congregated for worship from time to time, according to the order of the Society, until taken down in 1789; and here, too, some of the descendants of that fraternity domiciliated after the removal of the meeting-house, seeing that Samuel W. Fisher, a very respectable member of the Society of Friends, probably built and was located at No. 76, in a first-class three-story brick mansion of about forty feet front, with extensive yard and garden; a highly respected citizen and neighbor; bland, unassuming and plain, but of gentlemanly deportment.

This Mr. Fisher built the house in Arch street above Seventh in 1796, now the western part of the "Ashland House," which he, however, never occupied, but became the residence of Thomas W. McEwen, of the firm of McEwen, Hale & Davidson, and afterward of Bartholomew Wistar. The lot was seventy-four feet in Arch street, which gave to the house a side yard of about fifty feet. Its identity is incorporated in the "Ashland House," and the vacant ground on the west by two other large three-story bricks, in one of which, next above the hotel, we have our old merchant, John Farnum, and the other is now more varied in tenants as a boarding-house.

Leaving this digression and returning to my connection, I note another three-story brick on the Bank Meeting lot, next below Samuel W. Fisher, in the occupancy of Nathan Field, a bill-broker.

Mr. Field was a heavy man, of friendly mien, an adherent of the Society of Friends, and respectable in his calling.

The large house, No. 76, was built by *James* C. Fisher, the brother and partner of Samuel W. Fisher.

Here we have a companion of the old Quaker Meeting House, a relic of the olden antecedent of 1791, a two-story frame with porch and pent-house, the domicil and workshop of Benjaman Olden, boot and shoemaker.

My neighbor Olden was also of corporeal dimensions— not over-grown, but full· grown; a steady, quiet, well-disposed neighbor. But "Dick," his apprentice, often proclaimed a contrary opinion. "Dick" did not believe in early rising as a medium to health, wealth and wisdom, and therefore had to take the strap for his neglect of the lap-stone.

There was no six to six in those days, but daylight to dark was the law; and the "baas" required and demanded *all* the rights and privileges of the custom: sunrise was therefore a sad omen for "Dick" in bed, and his protest against the intrusion was apt to be loud and long.

But to the spot of my own beginning! An old time three-story brick intercepted the corner, and seemed to be squeezed in between that and the frame.

It was about sixteen feet front by fifty feet deep, with a nook of a shop in front, a small parlor annexed, and a strip of convenience for evening retirement in the rear, to which a corresponding strip of a yard outside gave the privilege of light and air, but the whole was hemmed in, surrounded, and out-topped by the wall of the corner and the Arch-street house, all which stretched along the side and rear of the lot.

This, though not my birth-spot, was the homestead of the first years of my existence, the humble domicil of my parents.

It was purchased of —— Lynch, in 1793, for £900 ($2400), where my father lived fifty-one years, until his demise on the 3d of November, 1834.

A familiar feature of the time was the frequent visits of Indians, some ring-nosed, feathered and painted, others in plain blanket, leggins and moccasins; a squaw or more in the rear as they marched listlessly on, with a papoose in a blanket secured to their back.

Most of the men had their bow and arrows, and proudly tested their skill upon "fip-penny-bits" stuck on edge on a chosen post—of which many ranged along the curb; their *aim* was but the precursor to the *game*, for they invariably hit the mark and took the prize, and that with the coldest indifference under a mere muscular monosyllabic utterance.

There is no more of this either; the posts are gone and the Indians approach us no longer in that familiar way.

Another peculiar feature of this early time offers itself to notice; as matter of by-gone curiosity, I perpetuate the fact: most of our streets were alive with swallows, which nestled under the eaves of the houses and came down morning and evening in rapid flight, up and down the street, skimming the ground in search of food, watched by the boys and but too often fell victims of their unerring clubs.

The march of improvement seems to have wiped that familiarity of the feathered tribe entirely out of the world's variety.

CHAPTER XXI.

A STRAY CHAPTER.

I MUST premise this chapter, by reference to, and correction
of, an error in my " History of the Moravian Church in Philadelphia," where, from an oversight of the proof-reader, I am
made to describe the *southeast corner of Second and Race* as
under demolition, instead of the NORTHWEST CORNER OF
FRONT AND ARCH, which was then—April, 1857—being
destroyed to its foundation.

This northwest corner of Front and Arch streets, was an
old-time affair, even in the year 1800.   It was of brick, three
stories on Front street, and three and a half on Arch street;
the second story on Front street was squared by a pent-house
and eaves, whilst on Arch street the third story showed up a
pediment from the eaves over the third story, which pediment
crowned the garret.

Its ground-plot was about twenty feet on Front street, by
some sixty or seventy on Arch street.   The main building

was about twenty by thirty, or at most forty feet deep; the rear portion on Arch street was two stories high, the second story of which, in 1804, was the culinary appendage to the upper part of the corner or main building.

This belonged to the Fisher family; and in 1791, and probably even beyond 1783, it was the store and counting-house of James C. & Samuel W. Fisher, who were shipping merchants of considerable note.

In 1802, it was in the occupancy of Hahn & Spohn, grocers, who begun business life here. The partnership was not of long duration. Mr. Spohn retired from the firm, and Mr. Hahn continued in very successful operation in the premises, having his residence up stairs for a season; the inconvenience of the confines, however, impelled a move to more convenient quarters; and he took them in Race, midway between Front and Second, south side.

It is but due to the memory of Mr. Hahn to say, that he was one of the most prominent and popular grocers of his day; unsurpassed in industry, and second to none in perseverance and attention to his business, in which he was *au fait* at all points. He took the tide of the times at its ebb, and rode its stream to its flood, where he made fast with the hawser of the wit and wisdom that bound him to the retreat.

Mr. Hahn was naturally a tall man, but a stoop or curve of his shoulders, from physical devotion to his business, reduced his erect measure.

The steadiness of his walk was the insignia of his purpose; it was straightforward, and thoughtful.

His countenance was intelligent, features sharp, nose aquiline and very prominent, lips thin and compressed, strong evidence of ability and determination to keep his own counsel; dark and rather listless eye, but marked and set in saga-

9

city; and but for the pits of small-pox, he was rather handsome than otherwise.

He left a large estate, and but one heir, a daughter, for its
benefits, who entered the matrimonial list with Dr. George B.
Wood, whose reputation for a liberal and proper disposition
of his monetary advantage, without ostentation, needs no illu-
mination whatever.

The money is in good hands.

My apprenticeship with Mr. Hahn, in 1804, gave me a full
scope for information of matters and things, for some distance
around my centre.

The whole of this, and the adjacent tenements north and
west, have been sunk in nonentity, and their identity worn off,
but for the privilege and the *penchant* of an antiquarian to review, resuscitate, and in memory perpetuate.

The march of improvement does not spare any thing; it
wipes up even the fastnesses of affection, and supplants the
fondnesses of antiquity; but it must and it *will* progress,
and it is for me only to show its ravages. Old times, to
" Young America," are of no account whatever; but, by-and-
by, " Young America," if it ever comes to *maturity*, will
covet a modicum of old time stability.

The march of improvement (in this case,) in its sway, has
obliterated the identity of the following constituents of this
corner and its neighbors.

First. On Front street, my own early homestead, No. 70.

Second. A well-built, modern three-story brick house, the
residence and dentistry of the late Robert Burkhard, who
built on Olden's lot, No. 72.

Third. Another good three-story brick, the former domicil
of Nathan Field, No. 74; thus clearing about eighty feet on
Front street.

Fourth. No. 13, on Arch street, adjoining the west end of the corner lot.

This was the happy home of Mrs. Widow Mary Sowerby, from whose hearth a bountiful supply of buckwheat cakes was served to the neighbors, every morning in winter, at six for sixpence; and her little shop in front was equally toothsome to young folks with burning pennies—apples, gingerbread, and candies being irresistible temptations to a flighty penny.

Mrs. Sowerby lived in this house for many years, from and after 1802.

Fifth. Savage Stillwell, merchant, in his day, 1805, enjoyed the retreat of No. 15. This was the grandsire of our present townsman, Mason Hutchins.

Sixth. Thomas Crumpston, merchant, and one of the Wardens of Christ Church, a rather austere old gentleman, was a member of the early community, at No. 17.

Seventh. John Claxton, ship-chandler, No. 19.

Eighth. The dignified and extensive domain of James C. Fisher—and, for many years after his removal, of his sisters Tabitha and Martha. No. 21—the numbers were very irregular—fell a "prey to the times."

This house covered some forty feet on Arch street, had a fine yard and garden, and stables in the rear, with ingress and egress through the arched alley in Front street, between Nos. 80 and 82, and known as Fisher's alley.

Ninth. Dr. Isaac Cathrall, a man of wit and pleasantry, eminent in his profession, a gentleman with protective force of sarcasm, if needed, was popularly known at No. 23; and here permit me to interpolate, that his wife, by maiden name, Kay, was perhaps the handsomest and finest-looking woman in the city at that time, 1805, and for many years after—aye,

even to her death; who, after her second union with Joseph
Worrel, and her third with David Jones, departed this life on
the 15th of June, 1858, in the seventy-eighth year of her age;
still stately and tasty in apparel, bearing all the delineations
of youthful beauty and continuous dignity of carriage.

To this point every vestige of old times has disappeared—
gone! forever gone!—ground to powder and mixed up with
the dust, and amalgamated in the pile that makes the levia-
than of the less ambitious owners of 1800.

I cannot refrain from a further digression at this point,
there being items of history in immediate connection with
this vicinity; nothing startling, but *ties* of the time—good
men of good manners, and active tributaries to the life of the
last, and beginning of the present century.

Amongst these, our respects are due to the memory of
Ambrose Vasse,* a prominent merchant, whose dwelling and
comptoir was the dignified mansion of No. 29, from 1794 to
1802; afterward, 1805, in the occupancy of Samuel Allen,
also a merchant; having stables and stores on the rear, accessible by Fisher's alley from Front street.

---

* Mr. Vasse was a Frenchman, and a respectable member of the Society of
Friends, and attended the Bank Meeting on the west side of Front street above
Arch.

He was a shipping merchant in good standing, but the French Revolution
crippled his finances, but not his respectability.

His title to the property above, came first by a bill of attainder to George
Haynes, March, 1778; afterward, Jared Ingersoll to Ambrose Vasse, 1794.

Tradition says, that this domain was the quarter of General Arnold, after
the battle of Saratoga; and that here his extravagance and indulgence over
his wound at Saratoga, brought him heavily in debt, and being refused by
Congress to make up his deficiencies, he hatched his scheme of treachery to
surrender West Point.

Mr. Vasse destroyed the old and perhaps *original* building, and erected the
mansion elsewhere noted in this volume.

William Gibbs, too, a retired merchant—blind for many years—was not without respectful notice at No. 31; whilst the famous Dickey Folwell pressed his wit, and sometimes his ribaldry, at No. 33, before he was located in Front street, as heretofore described.

Politics did not disrupt a man's household, nor command the business time of a partisan; for although our neighbor Benjamin Thaw gave active vent to his political opinions, he was none the less a very respectable tailor, at No. 37, mindful of his proper vocation, and successful in its pursuit.

Mr. Thaw was a gentlemanly and highly esteemed neighbor; his shop, or more technically, his shop-board, was in a one-story building next above his dwelling.

A passage of six or eight feet separated Mr. Thaw's shop from his dwelling, which was an avenue to one or two tenements on the rear, in one of which dwelt the well known Hannah January, a layer-out of the dead; she was the most popular official of that severe calling of that day.

Benjamin R. Morgan, attorney-at-law, was a prominent man at No. 41, in 1802, and sufficiently popular to be offered, by his political friends, after that time, as a proper incumbent of the gubernatorial chair of this State. In 1823, he was Judge of our District Court.

Mr. Morgan was a fine-looking man, tall, well-built, and wore his hair clubbed and powdered.

Our eminent Dr. Philip Syng Physic also contributed to the tone of wisdom, if not of wealth, at that time, 1795, of this neighborhood, No. 45.

This was in his celibacy. He afterward married a daughter of Samuel Emlen, an eminent member and minister of the Society of Friends.

Mr. Emlen died in 1799, in Arch below Sixth, on the premises—the minor part of which is the present office of your author, which office was also once that of Dr. Physic.

Dr. Physic died on the 15th of December, 1837, at the northeast corner of Union and Fourth streets, in the seventieth year of his age.*

Communities are necessarily made up of variety, and an incongruous mixture must, more or less, follow in the catalogue of subjects; and as recollections, particularly of a familiar spot, are difficult of control, the platform *will* show up any thing but kindred spirits—no disrespect to the contrast—but a mere representation of things as they were. Hence then let me pass to the other side of Arch street, and review and revive the life of that region down to the corner.

In this, I cannot pass the *odds* of society with the cold shoulder, nor link the time without a warm one to its more popular ends.

John Riddle, a tailor, of No. 34, on the south side, was a moving spirit of the time, a notorious draftsman on snuff, repudiating the box for the more spacious receptacle of his waistcoat pocket; and for his fancy obtained the title of "Snuffy Riddle."

Louis Gilliams, of No. 26, was perhaps the earliest dentist in Philadelphia; and was popular, for after 1795, he built a handsome three-story brick house on the opposite side, and was there eminent in his practice.

He was a full-sized man, of small voice, and of very pleasant

---

* The Doctor's residence, No. 45 Arch street, seems to have been not only a *source* of curative, but a current of the healing art, an apothecary shop having been there for many years; and even now is a mart for the benefit of the sick, under the proprietorship of Edward Gaillard, Jr., as No. 137, the successor of Thomas Dugdal, who was there from 1829.

and winning manners; pulled hard at a tooth, but beguiled the agony of his patient in the jocosity of his condolence. The old gentleman having served his day and generation, left his substance to his children, and his subjects to his son Jacob, who, after a time, moved to the more fashionable and more available quarters of Walnut street.

Another important "tin," showing the fears and terrors of a female under venesection, embellished the window-shutter of No. 24, of which Frederick Hailer, a small but venerable professor of phlebotomy, was the proprietor.

The pony of John Coburn awaited his master's will at the curb of No. 21, whence to his rigging-loft on the wharf, Mr. Coburn was borne daily.

Mr. Coburn was a snug little man, and his pony was well proportioned to his burden; they looked as if they had sought and found proportions.

Gustavus Risberg, a retired merchant, and a very clever man, was occupant of No. 16. It was a three-story brick, of respectable appearance—parlor somewhat elevated—and accessible by three or four stone steps running up sideways.

Mr. Risberg was resident here as far back as 1791, and until the early part of the present century, 1802–4.

Samuel Wetherill, Jr., occupied this house for several years afterward, which is still standing.

There is also yet standing—No. 12—a very weather-beaten, three-story brick tenement, of at least one hundred years durance.

In 1795 to 1805, Minia Brumige, a colored woman, and her aunt, or mother, known as "Old Phœbe," made and sold cakes and cranberry tarts at this point.

Brumige himself rather repudiated temperance pledges, which often made "midnight howl" over the controversy be-

tween Mrs. Brumige at the chamber-window, and Mr. Brumige
at the door below, on the difference of rheumatiz *vs.* rum-atiz,
doubtless to the great and oft-repeated annoyance of their
neighbor, John Goodwin, of No. 10, next door below.

In 1795, the popular and wide-known Humbert Droz,
made, repaired, and sold watches at this corner of Front and
Arch; but 1802 knew Joel Gibbs as manufacturer and vendor of hats, beaver, felt, and roram.

With a plea for indulgence for this curve in the order of
my detail, which I trust, however, is not altogether without
interest, I return to my proper line of march and observation.

Samuel Wetherill

CHAPTER XXII.

The East Side of Front street—Arch to Market—Samuel Wetherill, the Venerable Sire of the Fourth-rising Generation of that Family—John M. Taylor—Nothnagel & Montmollen—Saviel—Joshua Lippincott -Samuel York—Girard—Time of his Death.

RETURNING from my curve and its short compass, which I could not forego from its familiar characteristics and the face and features of the neighborhood, now for the most part non-existent, but sunk in the vortex of time, my Front-street review claims connection to my history, and the southeast corner of Front and Arch calls for its link to the Front street line.

Samuel Wetherill, the great-grandsire of the present generation, was the proprietor and owner of this southeast corner of Front and Arch, for some sixty or seventy feet southward from the corner, on the southern part of which there were, in 1791, two frames, one of which he owned and apparently nestled for future thrift; the other he bought of the elder Jacob Ritter, in 1793, and thus became the proprietor of what afterward loomed largely as No. 65; previous to this, however, he was located at No. 27 North Third street as druggist, apothecary and vendor of paints in colors.

Although a certain John Nicholson, Jr., gunmaker, occupied the corner in 1795, it is equally true that the Wetherills were the dominant parties in interest on that soil long before, the sire having planted his standard there over an embryo

pursuit even previous to 1791, whilst Samuel Wetherill &
Sons, druggists, oil and colormen, announce themselves at
No. 65 in 1795; and Mordecai Wetherill, one of the firm,
branched off in the same business at the corner, 1802, whilst
the like calling was found afterward for many years operative
by John Wetherill, another son, and Samuel Budd.

This concern was as of "acorn" growth—its branches were
vigorous and its foliage of healthy verdure even in the face
of time; and the notoriety of Samuel Wetherill & Son, druggists, oil and colormen, at No. 65 North Front street, like a
towering oak gilt by the sunshine of prosperity, stood defiant
of competition and regardless of the adverse winds of time
and circumstances; and as all this sprung from a very small
beginning, but a germ of intrinsic wealth, it is but a small
tribute to the memory of the elder Samuel Wetherill to present him as *that* germ; and I am happy in my ignorance of
any *family* pride that will frown or shy at the view of the
acorn, as it sprouted and spread its branches, growing fruits
of intrinsic value.

The ancestry of Samuel Wetherill originated in England,
and his immediate antecedents came to America and settled
in Jersey even before the arrival of William Penn. Mr.
Wetherill was originally a carpenter by trade, and as such
came to Philadelphia before the Revolution.

In process of time he changed his occupation from carpenter to that of weaver, and 'tis said, was the first weaver of
Jeans and Fustians in America, having his dwelling and
manufactory at No. 9 South alley, now Commerce street.

Here he made the best of time and circumstances; and
being a "Whig," and decidedly in favor of the defensive war,
made and sold materials for clothing the army, for which he
was disowned by the regular Society of Friends; but nothing

daunted, and being a man of very proper orthodox religious views, established at once another Friends' meeting, which, furthered by the liberality of the Legislature of Pennsylvania, by the donation and title of a lot at the southwest corner of Arch and Fifth street, enabled him, with several others of the same belief, to establish their independence in the building thereon erected, where also they were known as "Free Quakers," and by some the "Fighting Quakers"; here our Mr. Wetherill was the preacher until his demise. This property is still held by the Wetherill family.

His secular concerns, however, were in progress; and under date of April 3, 1782, I find the following advertisement in the "Pennsylvania Gazette":—

"Philadelphia Manufactures—suitable for every season of the year, viz.: Jeans, Fustians, Everlastings, Coatings, etc., to be sold by the subscriber at his dwelling-house and manufactory in South alley, between Market and Arch street and between Fifth and Sixth street, on Hudson's Square.

"Signed, SAMUEL WETHERILL."

In addition to this he carried on dyeing and fulling, at the same time nursing and coaxing up his *chemical* fancies; for even whilst thus engaged he was contriving other outlets for his genius.

His two-story frame and its lot, at No. 9 South alley, seems to have been the nursery and development of his inventions; for here his one-horse mill ground mineral secrets to powder, and his science analyzed their powers, virtues and effects, and at once tinted a popularity for the future.

Genius, nurtured by perseverance and furthered by industry, propitiated the smile of fortune, and upon her tide he rode to her very source, seeing that abundance crowned his enterprise.

Another mill in Coombs's alley planted his popularity there, and helped his development at No. 65, as before stated, where the firm of Samuel Wetherill & Son heralded the fame of the sire.

Samuel Wetherill, *Jun.*, here was the associate of his father, whom the genius of the parent followed; and *he* is said to have been the original in the manufacture of *White* Lead in this country. Certain it is that "Wetherill's White Lead" took the lead for many years, and *perhaps* even yet holds the palm; but to return to the sire:

His mansion and store was a *nonpareil* of his or even our time, and was an evidence of good architectural taste and the power that bore it to development.

It was a very handsome structure of brick, three stories in height, about thirty feet front and in depth to Water street. The store was on the front floor at an elevation of some three or four stone steps, a private entrance being on the north side of the store, requiring one or perhaps two more steps to its entrance to overcome the declivity that sunk the level to Arch street.

The parlor was on the second floor and the chambers of course above; and indeed in style and appearance had no superior for many a day after its erection. That, too, is sunk in the vortex of the march of improvement, and a vastly inferior new brick pile obliterates the dignity of its predecessor of 1793 to 1858.

It is, however, no charm of dollars and cents that gives *eclat* to the memory of Mr. Wetherill, but, rich or poor, there were cardinal virtues in the man. He was an *incorporation* of the better feelings of humanity; he possessed and practiced Christian virtues as well as moral duties, which I could trace to the days of the Revolution by good authority, but for the fear of some charge of unworthy motives; but to speak of his neighborly and brotherly kindness, benevolence, charity, and loveliness of manner, as amongst his practical virtues, outside of his business skill, tact and industry, is but a small compendium of his proper due.

I might say as much for his good lady, for her reputation will bear it; but that would be but a repetition of the character of her husband.

Mr. Wetherill was, as before stated, the founder of the Society of Free Quakers, whose meeting-house, built in 1783, still holds its own at the southwest corner of Fifth and Arch streets, where its founder and owner preached regularly until within a short time before his death, 1816.

They were often called "Fighting Quakers," not because they *did* fight, but because they thought self-defense was no transgression—they were not non-resistant.

In person he was of tall and handsome figure, with a marked index of his many virtues; the decrepitude of age, however, brought his wonted activity to the crutch, but his mental vigor gave nothing for time to feed upon.

Mrs. Wetherill was equally interesting in personal appearance, being of good figure, a tall and handsome woman.

They had three sons and one daughter, to wit: Mordecai, Samuel, John, and Sarah; and was perpetuated in his business first by his son Samuel, then by *his* son John Price and Dr. William, and now by John Price, the younger, associated with his uncle Dr. William Wetherill: the third generation thus lighting up the memory of a pioneer in Philadelphia's early business efforts, and a citizen worthy of all that I at least have said of him.

He was a native of Burlington, N. J., born there in April,

1736, and departed this life on the 24th of September, 1816, in the eighty-first year of his age.

And now leaving Mordecai Wetherill at the corner and his brother John and Samuel Budd in succession there, we have a narrow structure squeezed in between that and the mansion, a three-story brick of ancient date, in the occupancy of Dr. George Weed already in 1793, whence flowed the popular "Weed's Syrup," with other nostrums for the health and well-being of mankind in general.   No. 69.

Next below Wetherill's, No. 63, was another mansion of some dignity; though but a mere reflection of its neighbor, it was a first-class three-story brick, in the occupancy of John M. Taylor, a merchant, afterward a broker.   1802.

Mr. Taylor was the father-in-law of Hugh Calhoun, of the firm of Gustavus & Hugh Calhoun, eminent merchants of No. 37 North Water street, heretofore noted.

Nothnagel, Montmollen & Co. were eminent merchants in the occupancy of Nos. 61 and 63 in 1795, before the incumbency of Mr. Taylor of No. 63.

Passing a flight of steps to Water street (now closed), a little below, at No. 53, Tinee Cranshaw, a widow, and at No. 51 Samuel Saviel, both Africans, were fruiterers in 1795; but afterward, in 1808, these shanties were torn down and a large store was put up, and the bell of the well-known firm of York and Lippincott gave daily notice of a sale by auction on these premises.

They were the most prominent auctioneers of the day, and being very popular proprietors, they were beneficiaries of a large and profitable business.

These gentlemen were brothers-in-law, Mr. York having married Miss Lippincott.

Joshua Lippincott, was son-in-law to old Mr. Wetherill,

having married his only daughter Sallie.   He was a gentleman
of unassuming manners and popular for his urbanity, whilst
Mrs. Lippincott was an amiable participant of the best qualities of her parents—was well-beloved and highly esteemed,
as well as Mrs. Lippincott as she had been as Miss Sallie
Wetherill.

Joshua Lippincott died February 11, 1857, in his eighty-
fifth year.

Mr. Yorke was a prompt, active, and good business man,
of very dignified carriage, without *hauteur*, and was highly
esteemed as a merchant and a gentleman.   He died in 1815,
aged forty-two years.

In 1791, and long before, No. 43, at the south corner of
another flight of steps to Water street, our late opulent
Stephen Girard, was proprietor of a greengrocery, where
edibles to all tastes, from an onion to an apple and a bean to
a slice of pork, could be had for the money.   He occupied
through to Water street, and could sell at No. 31 there as at
No. 43 above.

Mr. Girard died December 26, 1831, in his eighty-fourth year; he was
therefore in his forty-third year in this embryo of his business life: hence,
we may fairly infer that Fortune kissed and embraced him after that time.

For particulars of Mr. Girard see pp. 71–76.

CHAPTER XXIII.

IN 1800, our present venerable George Thomas, now in his eighty-seventh year, was here in the full tide of merchandising; first under the firm of Thomas & Shreve, at No. 37, and afterward, 1805, associated with James Martin, under the firm of Thomas & Martin, at No. 45.

Mr. Martin is yet in harness, as a good, old-time merchant.

Mr. Thomas was not only a good merchant, but a good, available counselor to the business fraternity, dealing out advice liberally—and 'tis said wisely—so that he fairly earned the title of "the Front-street Lawyer."

Samuel, the father of the late William Sansom and Samuel Sansom, was here, at No. 45, in company with them, prominent and active in mercantile life, in 1802.

In 1791, John Clifford was a dealer in hardware at No. 39; but subsequently, Thomas and John Clifford continued the business under the firm of Thomas & John Clifford; they were, probably, the sons of Thomas Clifford, of No. 29 North Water street (1791), the proprietor of Clifford's wharf, and Clifford's alley, which opens here at No. 29.

They were ship-owners, and large importers of hardware

from Liverpool. The "Philadelphia," Capt. Bliss, was one of their ships in that trade, 1796, and long after.

The popular firm of Guest & Bancker were extensively engaged in the importation of British goods on the above premises, No. 39, in 1805; their importations were very heavy, compassing from £400,000 to £900,000 in a year.

In connection with this fact, I may state here, that in

1804 our foreign clearances were 618 vessels,
1805 "	"	"	"	617	"
1806 "	"	"	"	730	"
1807 "	"	"	"	712	"

Our foreign exports were, from Philadelphia,

1790	. . . . .	$17,523,866
1796	. . . . .	7,953,418
1809	. . . . .	9,049,421
1810	. . . . .	10,993,398

A master ship-builder of the time, states that, in 1810, there were 9,145 tons of shipping on the stocks.

The above statistic is from Dr. Mease's "Picture of Philadelphia," published in 1811.

Mr. Charles N. Bancker, the survivor of the firm of Guest & Bancker, is even yet our cotemporary; and though far advanced in life, proves himself a good business man to all intents and purposes.

He is, and has been from its beginning, the Secretary of the Franklin Fire Insurance Co., whose chair he occupied efficiently, and *from* its elbow is active beyond the years of an octogenarian.

In 1799, our familiar friend, Samuel Archer, began his fortune in the purchase and sale of East India muslins, at No. 35, where his trade increased and drove him from these limits

10

to wider borders; and No. 28, on the opposite side, heralded him as an extensive importer of East India goods.

Fortune here smiled upon his efforts, and wealth crowned his labors; but fortune afterward frowned him into the chill shades of adversity, and left him a victim to her caprice.

He deserved, as far as we can see, a better issue, for he was a worthy, unassuming citizen. Untainted of *hauteur*, the zenith of his prosperity was but as the horizon of his *debut*, and none felt any difference of his *maximum* in contrast with *their minimum*.

Amongst his employees, we trace the father of our Morris L. & Joshua Hallowell, of the firm of M. L. Hallowell & Co., of No. 333 Market street, who, after his services to Mr. Archer, made a voyage to Canton, and on his return became a mercantile spirit of the day on his own account.

This same No. 35 was, in 1802, the business spot of Joseph Cooper, a dry goods merchant—a plain, unsophisticated gentleman, of kindly manners, of enviable repute, and popular in the business and the social circle; he lived in this house.

He was the sire of the generation continued with our Dr. Collin C. Cooper, a grandson.

A golden lamb, over the door of No. 25, looking northward, heralded the whereabouts of Mrs. Jane Taylor, whose reputation as a dealer in dry goods and trimmings, begat for her a pleasing and lucrative patronage.

A very fixture was William Hembel, a bachelor, at No. 17, even from 1791 to far into the present century.

Mr. Hembel was not only a merchant, but a fondler with the medical science, and was esteemed as well for his *curative* wisdom, as he was for the current duties of his counting-house. He was calm, cool, and deliberate of time's privileges, and very philosophically took the world as he found it.

He was President of the Academy of Natural Sciences; died 12th June, 1851, aged eighty-seven years, and was buried at Laurel Hill.

Our very eminent barrister, David Paul Brown, sprung to existence at No. 11. His father, Paul Brown, being a merchant tailor on this spot, in 1795; and the son David, an embryo *literati*, after absorbing the pith of his accumulations of various minds in print, disposed of them from a case at the door.

Henry Tremper, afterward more extensively engaged in the dry goods business on the west side, and of whom more in the next chapter, offered his wares in 1800, at No. 7; but amongst the variety of dry goods, shop, or store-keepers, there was none better known than Mrs. Hannah Holland, at No. 3.

Mrs. Holland was very popular for her easy manner, and liberal allowance for an adverse opinion of a customer—always happy if they bought, and content if they did not.

She was of very extensive proportions, heavy, and doubtless very inconvenient to herself, but sufficiently active in her store duties. Wealth settled upon her, and she settled it upon her only child—a daughter—afterward Mrs. Singleton.

Mrs. Holland was the widow of Benjamin Holland, who occupied Nos. 3 and 5, in 1791, in the dry goods trade, which Mrs. Holland continued at No. 3, in and from 1802.

It is, however, something more than a reminiscence, to trace a worthy cotemporary to his place of beginning.

Our William R. Thompson, after a reasonable apprenticeship with his uncle, John Thompson, of Second and South streets, set out for himself in the grocery trade, at this northeast corner of Front and Market streets, in 1812.

Mr. Thompson being still amongst us, needs no representative or delineator of character; his bland, open, and honest manner being but the concomitant of a countenance of un-mistakable integrity. He is an Irishman by birth, but a valuable American citizen in all his practice.

John T. Sullivan occupied the up stairs (second story) of this store, as a book-bindery. His work was of the best sort, and his blank-books for the counting-house, accordingly ex-pensive—but they were durable. Mr. Sullivan was active in doors and out: in the one at the "press," and at the "polls" in the other, for he was withal a lively politician.

I cannot, however, leave this point without a reflex of an eccentric who had a way of his own somewhere in the square, about the years 1785 to 1790.

George Frederick Boyer, cutler, a German, was a man of small stature, supporting, however, a mind fraught with that variety that floats on the atmosphere of visions, but with un-compromising nationality moulded his conceptions into stub-born facts.

He was a German Lutheran by profession, but in many re-spects a Swedenborgian in practice; and this he exemplified in the arrangement of a room, furnished, but kept sacred for the assembling of the "Christian Society," which consisted of the twelve apostles; besides this, a plate or more, with knife, fork, and napkin, and chair in front, at and of his din-ner-table, were for the silent presence of one or more expected guests from the world of spirits. Other *mortal* guests, how-ever, did not fare so well; for, on one occasion, a *real* individ-ual came to dine with them, and brought his dog with him, but the dog's modesty kept him at the door. His master missing him, called out, "Luther! Luther!" "What!" says Mrs. B., "Luther! after whom, pray?" The man answered, carelessly, "Dr. Luther." "Dr. Martin Luther!" exclaimed she, indignantly, at the same time giving the dog a kick and a thrust to his master, saying: "The ever-blessed Dr. Martin Luther be gone!" That man lost his dinner.

His spiritual intercourse was not confined to his *sanctum*, nor his ordinary; but the upper kingdom recognized him, and pictured his initials in stars, which he asserted he had seen with mortal eye, and so reported in his diary—which I saw some years ago—in the form of a quadrate of a circle, studded with stars, with "G. F. B." in large type in the centre.

Though small in form and feature, he abjured comparison or allowance for his measure, and very indignantly repulsed the kindly consideration of his shoemaker, when he offered a deduction on account of the smallness of his foot.

He was no less tenacious of his right, title and interest in his domicil, which, during his ownership, he used to his liking, and went whithersoever he would; but, in process of time, he sold his house to William Folwell, and fell sick and bed-ridden with consumption. His cough was troublesome, and expectoration frequent; but, being no longer the owner, he refused the benefit of the soil, and spite of his wife's entreaties to "spit out," he would crawl to the window to discharge the incumbrance.

Although Mr. Folwell was a very clever and kind-hearted man, G. F. B. could not bear his presence, nor the sound of his foot, which, being deformed, was a contorted vision—at this time—to his unhappy brain.

He was one of Nature's oddities, but by no means deranged.

Mr. and Mrs. Boyer were alike small, but no less consequential than larger folks; and it must have been amusing to see them, on their way to church, stop short at intervals, face each other, and thus hold a conversation.

Despite the mixture of *his* creed, *she* was a rigid Lutheran, and turned an invited guest out of her house, as heretofore given, for desecrating the name of her patron saint.

All of the foregoing is from reliable tradition—a cotemporary intimately acquainted with the parties. But, this authority having long since departed, I cannot trace his *spot ;* but my details are the birth of a tenacious memory, unmistakably impressed, for at least forty years. Please, therefore, accept it for whatever it is worth.

CHAPTER XXIV.

In 1802, this southwest corner of Front and Arch streets, was the hatter-shop and manufactory of Joel Gibbs.

The workshop was in the cellar, open on Arch street, where I have often seen the men around the boiling caldron, dipping and withdrawing the felts in commendable haste, to save their own skin from the scald, rolling the felt as they withdrew it on the inclined plain, or plank slope, to the mouth of the kettle, having leather palms protective of the infliction of every successive dip.

These kettles, or caldrons, were encased in brick-work over a furnace below, surrounded at the top by a sloping ledge of two-inch plank, of twelve or eighteen inches in width, of quadrangular or sexangluar form, so that each man might have his place.

Peruquiers were as necessary, though perhaps not as important in those days, as they are now, and belonged to the assortment of life's busy scenes; and the widow, Mrs. George Taverner, was no less desirable to ladies whom nature had neglected, than Joel Gibbs was to gentlemen, to top off their fancies.

Wigging, braiding, and hair-dressing being the *forte* of Mrs. Taverner, hers was the seat of popularity, next below the hattery of Joel Gibbs, and there ladies, cut unkindly by dame Nature, debarred the pleasure of combing and arranging their own hair, resorted for the compensatory skill of Mrs. Taverner. 1800.

Her husband, however, was here in 1795.

At this period, 1795, Thomas Peacock at No. 64; Cornelius Comegys, No. 62; Baker & Comegys, No. 60; and William Lippincot, the father of Joshua Lippincot, at 56 and 58, were all prominent and active merchants: they were the life of trade, and gave tone to their quarters.

But after this, in 1802, *the* Tinman of the day, Conrad Keller, bestrode the domain of No. 64, and rung the welkin with the vibration of tin under the mallet.

Indefatigable and industrious himself, his boys were entirely bereft of any indulgence; and what the word of command failed in, the cowhide enforced—a usual convincing argument of the day, and one that often told far and wide, by the ring of the material under the active mallet of his young disciples, from the cellar—the central point of his employees long before the sun woke up day in the winter season.

Mr. Keller was a German, and a rigid disciplinarian, but some of his boys were wags; and as he often prefaced his intentions of castigation by taking a hearty pinch of snuff, or found use for one of his hands and kerchief for a more sonorous enunciation, his subject would slip his grasp and escape to bed, if at night, or the bench, if in the morning—for this was generally a morning or evening exercise.

"Soll I cut-ee: oder soll I hau-ee?"* was the fearful,

---

* "Shall I *whip*, or *flay* you?"

threatening interrogatory; but I never heard of any one being hurt; the manner was more than the matter. This old neighbor was faithful to his bench, and his treasury told of the fruits of his industry.

He lived long, and died rich.

Harvey & Worth were prominent and very popular dealers in hardware, for many years after 1802, at No. 62.

Mr. Harvey was eminent for consistent piety; and Mr. Worth, in keeping with his name, a worthy citizen of untarnished character.

Delving a little into the last century, touching 1795, the following array of mercantile life claims recognition:

John Folwell, at No. 52.

George Justice and Joseph Cooper, at No. 48.

David Knox and James Henderson, No. 46.

George Eyre, No. 40, and Marc Praeges & Co., No. 36, were all active constituents of the business life here; and our staid and steady, benevolent Friend, John Thomas, too, at No. 32, was a highly esteemed neighbor, and an amiable principal of his store, a neat, tidy, and unassuming Quaker gentleman; and no less so his next neighbor, No. 30, of No. 110, near Race, to wit: Henry Drinker, Jr., whose presence at No. 110, has already been revived.

This John Thomas was, at one time, 1805, the partner of Thomas P. Cope, under the firm of Cope & Thomas, No. 19, North Second street.

There was a *very extensive* crockery store and warehouse at No. 24, giving very busy life to the neighborhood. The front store was large and capacious, but a wide passage or carriage-way inserted the block on the south, and led to the warehouse and stables in the rear.

John Morrel was the very popular proprietor of this concern, and was justly esteemed for his urbanity, which his personal appearance endorsed.

He was a gentleman of the old school; wore powder, but no particular fashionable cut of apparel.

His carriage and pair bore him whithersoever he would; and prosperity greased its wheels and fattened his horses.

Morrel was the largest crockery dealer of that day, in Philadelphia.

In 1791 he was at No. 23, on the opposite side; but, in 1793, we find him as a China merchant—far ahead of the refinement of our day—as above, at No. 24; but he was a fixture there for many years, for I write now with my eye on him, some time after 1800.

Thomas Wotherspoon was well known at No. 22. Garrison & Taylor, at No. 20, and Nathan Folwell at No. 16, were prominent dry goods merchants in this compass; and James Potter, at No. 8, but afterward more prominent in Market street, near Sixth, on the south side, was probably in embryo here.

James Arrot was afterward the incumbent of this No. 8, in 1805, and flourished extensively and prominently.

The nucleus of the Josiah White family, Solomon White, was here, in the dry goods trade, at No. 6.

This was the father-in-law of Josiah White, of Lehigh Navigation memory, and the lord of the country-seat of about four acres, at what is now Eleventh and Callowhill streets, where the mansion stood transverse on the farm, facing the Delaware, and where this sire and his domestic associates enjoyed the pleasures of rural felicity. And here, too, our own Josiah White found a helpmate of kindred spirit, to carry out a life of benevolence, and spread their bounty without stint, amongst deserving mendicity.*

It is but common justice to the memory of Josiah White, and his Mrs. White—as he thus presents himself in connection with his father-in-law in my proper range—to record him as one of the most benevolent men of our age—whose study in life was benevolence, and *security* in death for its continuance.

There was, however, other important life in this square, for besides the skill of William Widdifield, at No. 46, and William Cox, at No. 50, both in the art of chair-making, there were five hatters in the row; and the memorable musk-rat crouching over the door of No. 44, denoted the calling of William Gerhard there, even from 1795 to forty years thereafter.

This shop was at the south corner of Coombs's alley. It was originally a one-story tenement, but the grading of the street threw up the cellar-wall and exalted the humble feature of architecture to top, and dignify its former subordinate, and thus made a two-story building.

This spot seems to have been the summit of the square; the elevation of the rear of this and its neighboring buildings, showed a slope north to Arch, and south to Market street, so that the houses, large or small, originally stood high in mid-air.†

Isaac Norris, too, was a very respectable member of the same fraternity, at No. 42.

---

* There is not a tree nor a shrub left to mark this domain; Callowhill street and Eleventh street squares the farm, and brick piles hedge, block, and encumber the freedom of light and air, that but a little while ago, had fair play to sing and smile through the open domain of Solomon White.

† The elevation from the Delaware, high tide, was about twenty feet.

Mr. Norris was an active, intelligent, and industrious man, and with his neighbor, Joseph Kay, near by, gained and obtained the respectful considerations of a popular patronage.

Besides these, John Sykes, at No. 38, and Benjamin Cooper, at No. 54, were at the service of any customer for a good hat.

But the line was assorted. Tallow, dips, and moulds were as important to the *salon* as they were at the *boudoir*, and somebody must make them; mechanics or manufacturers were not so far below par as to be lost in their vats, or metamorphosed at the bench, or the store.

Thomas Wishart and William Wishart were a pair of respectable bachelors, and eminent tallow chandlers, at the south corner of Pewter Platter alley—now called Jones's alley —and Front street. 1802.

They were of the Society of Friends, and in demeanor characteristic of their profession, tame, modest, and retiring, faultless to the human eye, except their repudiation of marital discipline. They ought to have united, even at a risk, for a share of the "better or worse" of the matrimonial contract; else they were proper men, and were well spoken of.

Frugality was no doubt a cardinal point in their domestic economy, of which their housemaid seems to have been sufficiently imbued.

Failures, in those days, were few and far between—yet they did occur, and often were ascribed more to extravagance than misfortune.

One of the unfortunates happened to be a neighbor, and "Betty" discovered the cause at the bake-house; for on her return with their savory portion, she told the bachelor brothers that it was no wonder that friend J. had broke, for their pudding smelt uncommonly strong of orange-flower water. Tommy and Billy Wishart did not indulge in this kind of odor.

They were both of medium stature, and not over-burdened with flesh and blood; but their neighbor of No. 12, perhaps equalized the proportions, seeing that Joseph Shoemaker was equal to both together in size and weight.

Mr. Shoemaker was a prominent and popular silversmith there; and for many years before and after 1799, contributed to the busy scenes and doings of Front near Market street.

Edward Rewley, more prominent in after-times, stepped from No. 7, on the east side, to No. 10, on the west, and furthered his interests by his own skill in buying and his wife's in selling, for she had the reputation of being a first-rate saleswoman. 1802.

CHAPTER XXV.

Front street, East side—Market to Chestnut—Ephraim, Benjamin and Ellis
   Clark—John Vernou—James McCrea—John McCrea—C. F. Roussel—
   Shoemaker & Berrel—John Gill—Daniels & Phillips—John Hood—Patrick
   Moore—Blair McClenechan—Joshua B. Bond—Joseph R. Tatem—Tarrascon
   & Journel—Brugiere & Tessiere—James Duval.

So early as 1791, our late venerable friend and townsman,
Ephraim Clark, was established as a watchmaker at the southeast corner of Front and Market streets.

He was succeeded by his brother Benjamin; and then again
Benjamin and Ellis Clark kept up the line and the location
for many years. They were brothers of John Clark, of Arch
and Water street, all of whom were highly respectable and
good citizens.

The life of gossip is said to be in a barber-shop, there news
gather and thence scatter, and John Vernou, a Frenchman, of
No. 3, had the advantage of the ruminations of wit, wisdom,
and report; and if he had not the credit of *enlightening* the
community, he certainly had that of being the centre of at-
traction, to which his "poll" gave the silent but significant
call.

This, though a notch in the *mercantile* line, belongs to the
score of the life of the times; and although John Vernou's appendages were not exactly merchantable, they certainly were

marketable to those to whom a razor or scissors were a desideratum. All this apart.

We have even now a most indefatigable and valuable citizen, uncompromising to misfortune, and unyielding to adversity, in the person, character, and indomitable perseverance of John McCrea; whose root we trace to No. 5, here, in the retired James McCrea, who had passed the ordeal of mercantile life, and rested upon his laurels already, in 1799.

This Mr. McCrea was an importer of Irish linens—an item of considerable importance in his day. There were, however, other very respectable sources of trade in this connection.

C. F. Roussel, a French merchant, at No. 7.

Shoemaker & Berrel were insurance brokers, at No. 9. This Jacob Shoemaker was a heavy-built man, and was well known far into the present century.

William Smith, Jr., No. 13.

John Gill, No. 15.

Daniels & Phillips, No. 25.

John Hood, No. 27, and Patrick Moore, No. 33, were alike active spirits of 1795, and after; they all sold and bought, and, for the most part "got gain." But Blair McClenechan, a familiar friend of your author, in his very green youth, was also here, at No. 33, in 1795.

Mr. McClenechan was a public-spirited gentleman, lighting up the shades of his mercantile meanderings with the rays of some star of hope, for the prosperity of his adopted State or city, for Mr. McClenechan was an Irishman; one of his stars was the Easton Delaware Bridge, which he, with others, warmed to life, by untiring time and attention to the lottery that sprung the arches and the pass from Pennsylvania to Jersey.

He was a manager of that lottery; and, as a boy, I have

seen him sit at the table below the wheels of Fortune, announcing fate, as he clipped the thread of the small-rolled
ticket, and told its secret.[*]

This rotund old gentleman justly belongs to the tenacity
of grateful recollections, for his benefits to public as well as
private life; but I must leave him for some other page of history, and pass on to my line of march.

After Joshua B. Bond, of No. 39, and Joseph R. Tatem, of
No. 49, the popular French firm of Lewis Tarrascon & Victor
Journel, held forth in the silk trade, at No. 51; they were
amongst the earliest importers of French silk goods, and were
extensively and profitably engaged in the trade for many
years after 1795.

The firm of Brugiere & Tessiere, of Market street, in 1805,
and onward, in the same business, grew out of that of Tarrascon & Journel, Charles Brugiere having been clerk and sales-
man for them, and doubtless well informed of the art and
mystery of ordering and buying and selling silks, long and
short, under a proper tariff, associated with Anthony Tessiere,
in like capacity; with our well-known and friendly James
S. Duval, then gathering himself up by the same means, first
at No. 80 North Second street, 1805, but subsequently, in
1807, more extensive and progressive at No. 153, and thence
to No. 179 Market street.

---

[*] This lottery was drawn in Independence Hall, by two boys of ten years
of age, perched on a large table, before a large box-wheel, from which, after
a turn or more, by a crank, they—opening a small door in its side—drew a
single ticket, held it up to general view, and then handed it to the manager
below, who clipped the thread, and audibly proclaimed the secret of the
roll.

The boys were dressed in a blue suit, trimmed with gold, or tinsel lace,
with sleeves tight to the arms, and bound at the wrists with the lace, to bar
suspicion of fraud or deception.   1800 to 1802.

These were all three highly reputable firms, progressive from first to last; but Brugiere & Tessiere progressed out of our limits; and, as before stated, were amongst the first of our merchants to leave the confines of Philadelphia, thus helping to build up New York,—a small affair of an emporium in 1815.

11

CHAPTER XXVI.

THIS southwest corner is too well known for any perpetua-
tion of mine, but my catalogue of life in its range calls for
reference to its incumbent of 1795; but James Stokes, in his
looking-glass dealings, was as well known then, and long in
after life, as the premises. He was certainly a thrifty merchant, for he left considerable land-marks; but he was as well
a thrifty Christian, and left his mark, of a godly sort too,
and the individual that met him by the way had need of a
durable button-hole to hear him out, for he let no one go
without a witness.

Thomas Bradford, the root of the present generation of that
name, was prominent as a bookseller, and editor of the newspaper called the "True American," at No. 8.

This was a very old and original affair of a building; narrow, perhaps not over sixteen feet front, and any thing but
convenient. It was sold, after his time there, to our very
popular and familiar John Moss, (who could not have had
much trouble to tear it down,) and he put up a store in its
place.

I cannot pass this name—although it is out of my limits—without a respectful memento.

This Mr. Moss was an Israelite, a man of probity, upright and benevolent, and highly esteemed in all his relations in life: amiable, affable, and familiar.

His *fac simile*, in person and character, is well defined in his son, Joseph L. Moss, our fellow-citizen of Spruce street.

Mr. John Moss was an Englishman, born in London, in 1771, and came to the United States in 1793.

His beginning in trade was small, but his perseverance was progressive; and his uncompromising probity and winning manners begat for him a popularity that handed him up to an enviable position in mercantile life.

In process of time, his borders increased, and his business spread from his adopted to his native country, of which his ships "Moss" and "Tontine" were periodical heralds.

Steadiness of pursuit, and unwavering integrity, paid their way, and crowned his decline with a golden sunset; for in addition to a very desirable reputation, social or public, his own vine, and his own fig-tree, shaded and nourished his latter day, and eased him from the theatre of mortal life.

But the turning point of his weal, or woe, was incidental to the war of 1812.

After selling out his stock of dry goods, in Market above Fourth, to the late William S. Crothers, in whom his confidence induced a credit of from one to four years, he went to London, with letters of introduction to Bainbridge & Brown, whose confidence he gained to a full ratio of credit if needed.

Goods of all description were plenty and cheap there, and scarce and high here. A *coup de main* presented itself as his crank of the wheel of Fortune; and "I'll risk all I have, some sixty thousand dollars," said he to B. & B., "and load a ship for America." At once he went into the purchasing of almost every variety of English manufacture; which, however, far exceeding his own means, was borne out by his friends Bainbridge & Brown.

This done, he came home in a cartel, to await the arrival of his "Brilliant"; but tedious and anxious was his waiting; sixty, seventy, and onward to eighty days passed, and no "Brilliant"—the gauntlet must be run! Could she escape? Doubts and fears beset him and his friends, yet some were willing to buy him out, ranging from seventy down to fifty thousand dollars for the cargo. As time narrowed her chance, "Keep your nerve," said his wife, though poverty was pinching her and her charge. He took the hint; the sun of the seventy-ninth or eightieth day gilt the shrouds of the "Brilliant" as she came round the point below, and *secured* his golden sunset.

The cargo was sold at public auction, and yielded him a profit of two hundred and fifty thousand dollars; thus Fortune took him by the hand ·and led him to her treasury.

Mr. Crothers paid his paper—sixty thousand dollars. Bainbridge & Brown, theretofore strangers to him, lent him their confidence; and the providence of God allowed his ship to pass the ordeal of squadrons, privateers, and blockade; but to his credit be it recorded, none of these things marred his usual good behavior.

After this his counting-house was at No. 75 South Front street, where he continued as a shipping merchant, from 1816 to 1828, when he retired from mercantile pursuits.

Mr. Moss was not only useful to himself, but was so, more

or less, beyond the limits of his *comptoir*. He served in our City Councils, in and after 1830, and was there amongst the most estimable of his companions; and his general liberal views rendered him always available. But I am not here to biographize or eulogize. I knew him personally, and am happy in this opportunity to pay the foregoing, as but a just tribute to his memory.

He died April 5th, 1847, aged seventy-six years.

Passing this interregnum, my regular course thus presents itself.

The "True American" was sold out to Thomas T. Stiles, and passed from him to *nonentity*.

John Taylor, an insurance broker, was the busy life of No. 10.

This Mr. Taylor was the father-in-law of our recent cotemporary, John Strawbridge, a very intelligent gentleman and merchant of the day. 1795.

Our present citizen of Germantown, John Magoffin, represents the former firm of Joseph Magoffin & Son, merchants, of No. 12. 1795.

Benjamin Nones, a highly respectable Hebrew, was favorably known as a dealer in dry goods, and celebrated for vending Madras handkerchiefs, at No. 14; he was afterward appointed Notary Public in 1795, and many years after.

This square was lively in merchandising, of whose operators a synopsis here may suffice—to wit:

Wilson Hunt, No. 16; Anthony Kennedy, No. 18; Meeker, Cochran & Co., No. 20; John Field, No. 24; Joseph D. Drinker, at the same number; and James Todd and William Mott, were at No. 26; but from this point there were others more prominent and more generally known. Mazurie & Homaffel were prominent French merchants, at No. 28, in 1791; continued, however, far into the present century, by James Mazurie.

James Donath, too, a German merchant, occupied the same premises with Mr. Mazurie, in 1795. Mr. Donath was highly respectable in his calling, and a very estimable citizen.

But there was busier life than all this in this line—and what can be more so than a city post-office? Here Robert Patton, at No. 36, administered to public curiosity, as well as to the commercial interests of the day, in the constant distribution of letters and other documentay inditings, to the dense and doubtless often clamorous gathering.   1793.

This office had been at No. 7, on the opposite side, under the same post-master, in 1791.

Our present venerable Jonah Thompson, in his tenure of life, yet represents the house of his father, John Thompson, of No. 38, in 1791, an importer and vendor of dry goods; whilst the father of our late John Stille, Jr., and Benjamin Stille,—Mr. John Stille, Sr., tailor,—a worthy citizen, was popular in his calling, at No. 40.

Mr. Stille and his good lady were a pious pair, good Presbyterians, and estimable members of the Arch-street meeting, northwest corner of Third and Arch streets.

Alexander Henry, from No. 17 South Second street, in 1791, moved mercantilely here, at No. 42, in 1793.

Mr. Henry was as well known in this century as in the last. He was a prominent man in the importation of Irish linens, and other British dry goods, and an eminent man in hospitalities, charities, and benevolence.

He afterward had his store, and resided in Market street, south side, next below the corner of Sixth street, in a very handsome, first-class, three-story brick house, remarkable for its semicircular marble steps, two and a sill, to the private entrance.

This is the root of our present very gentlemanly Mayor, who is a son of John S. Henry, late a merchant on the Market street premises, as successor to his father, the subject of this notice.

CHAPTER XXVII.

The East side of Front street—Chestnut to Walnut—Ephraim Clark—Peter
S. Duponceau—Richard Footman—N. McVicker—Loup—Walker—Reed—
Ford—Rubb—Frazier—Joseph Roberts: Appearance and Character—
Thomas Biggs—John McCauley.

In 1791 Ephraim Clark was, as before stated, at the southeast corner of Front and Market street, but in 1793 he was at this southeast corner of Front and Chestnut, as watchmaker at No. 55.

Our late venerable Peter Stephen Duponceau ranged here at No. 59, in 1793. Mr. Duponceau was an eminent jurist, a man of letters, and literary to a fault, far beyond the cover of a book. He seemed to forget every thing, even his own name escaped his recollection; but withal he was one of the most interesting men of the age, plethoric of literary lore and always happy in the dispensation of his literary wealth. His snuff-box and his tome were boon companions, but in conversation a hearty pinch of snuff seemed to elasticize his memory and quicken its issues.

He was peculiar in manner; a gentleman, but trammeled with very imperfect vision, so that two pairs of spectacles were important to him—"to look before you leap." I have often seen him put on his second pair to be satisfied of his opposite party.

He was of rather heavy physiognomy, but vivid in effect, dark complexion, very evidently thinking brow, and a full head of hair. He walked always in deep thought, and must needs be addressed or arrested to recognize a passing acquaintance. His *sortie* was deliberate, and marked by the folding of his wrists behind him and the bend of his shoulders, as if borne over by the weight of his mental meanderings.

In 1802 he was the lord of the manor of the northeast corner of Sixth and Chestnut streets, where, from his mansion at the corner, he retired to his literary sanctum on the rear, defended by a brick wall from the vulgar *bruit* of a public highway.

Besides his legal and literary attainments and consequent duties, Mr. Duponceau was in early times, 1793, a Notary Public and interpreter of foreign languages, in which he was doubtless of the first class.

He was a gentleman of the old school, and always at home in good manners despite his absence of mind.

He died March 31, 1844, aged eighty-four years.

Merchandising was vested in other parties, which the thread of my history again reunites. For Mr. Duponceau was not a merchant, but a lawyer. He was, no doubt, often the bosom of commercial ills. He certainly was a recipient of spare funds, for though a Huguenot refugee, he did not die poor; it was said of him that on one occasion, in a prize case, he received a fee of ten thousand dollars. But to my merchants, and of them the catalogue runs thus:—

Richard Footman was auctioneer at No. 65. Nathan McVicker, merchant, No. 67. John Loup, a French merchant, No. 71. Emanuel Walker, No. 73. John Reed and Standish Ford, No. 91. John and Wm. Rubb, No. 93; and Nalbro and John Frazier, merchants, of No. 95.

Here we trace a well-known and respectable citizen, grown into popular favor by time, circumstances and good manners.

Joseph Roberts was the apprentice and clerk to this last firm, whence he became a clerk in the original "Bank of the United States"; and thence, after its close, an official and efficient helpmate to Girard in his banking operations, where he continued to its close, and wound up his life in winding up the affairs of his early employer, the original United States Bank of 1791.

Although the serious, sober countenance of Mr. Roberts was not exactly attractive, yet his manner was a negative to timidity—his apparent reserve was but the guardian of his self-respect, for whether as master or man, his intercourse was civil, respectful, and gentlemanly.

His remarkably erect stature and his measured gait, seemed to be outward evidence of inward possessions; his very "queue" seldom swerved from the line of its privilege.

I have had business intercourse with him in all of his various public stations in life; and whether as clerk, cashier or trustee, I never saw him, or heard of his losing his balance of decorum. He was a gentleman of the old school, and never lost any thing due to the character of a gentleman, from his clerkship to his trusteeship.

He died at the age of eighty-one years, on the 23d of April, 1856.

Thus much to the memory of Mr. Roberts. I proceed with the thread of my history. The ways and means of sustenance were not confined to mercantile pursuits; the mechanic arts must have claims to *localie* as well as respectful patronage.

Mathematical instruments were important to business life, and Thomas Biggs of No. 81, in 1793, and for many years after, was a popular leader in that profession, in which he was eminent, and resident in this neighborhood for many years.

Coppersmiths, too, were not without the respectful patronage due to their calling; and Mr. John McCauley of No. 89 (1791, afterward 1805 at No. 119 South Front), was no less notorious in that capacity than the shipper that skirted the water in his rear; but Mr. McCauley, tired of the non-elastic din of copper tones, and perhaps for a more extensive mental outlet or active pedal movement, abandoned that art for the arts and mysteries of brokering, and established himself as broker in Dock street. Mr. McCauley married the sister of our distinguished Commodore Stewart, and was therefore the brother-in-law to the Commodore. He was a tall, limber, and active —but not quick—mover in life, bending a little forward from his shoulders, well known to many of our citizens even into later times.

CHAPTER XXVIII.

Front Street—West Side—Chestnut to Walnut—P. Hartshorne—Ebenezer
Large—Sitgreaves—Orr—Evans—Fox—Robert Smith—John Elliot—Wil-
liam Geisse—Dr. Griffiths—John Dixon—Jonathan Fell—Daniel King—
John Connelly—Samuel Coates—Roberts Vaux.

PATTISON HARTSHORNE and Ebenezer Large were the
active spirits in the wholesale dry goods trade at this southwest corner; and the line southward for some distance, to wit:
from No. 46 to No. 60, was kith and kin in like pursuits, for
here John Sitgreaves was sought in the capacity of a dry
goods merchant at No. 48.

Thomas Orr, in like request at No. 52, and John E. Evans
& Co. at No. 54, told out their dry goods and the inducements
to a liberal patronage, although in those days special plead-
ings were altogether unnecessary. The vendors were respect-
ively and respectably known, and needed neither "Herald"
nor "Drummer" beyond a respectful newspaper notice of their
whereabout. But the clang of an auctioneer's bell occasion-
ally shattered the quiet of the neighborhood, to announce a
public sale by Edward Fox, at No. 56; and this auction mart
was an insertion in the line.

This No. 56 was variously occupied by John Connelly,
Hacker, Brown & Co. (our David S. Brown), and finally, in
1829, became the property and drug mart of the late Nicholas
Lennig, of whom Charles Lennig and Frederick Lennig are
even yet his successful successors. Nicholas Lennig was a

German, a man of industry and enterprise, and his fruit, lateral and collateral, have not fallen far from the tree.

Mr. Nicholas Lennig came to this country in 1819, began in a small way, and died in 1835, in his forty-seventh year, leaving a good business and a good balance-sheet.

Robert Smith, however, took up the line next below at No. 58, and pursued a popular and profitable trade in dry goods for many years; for Robert Smith was well, wide and popularly known here even in 1795, and more than twenty-five years after.

Here the scene varies materially. Drugs nor pharmaceuticals were legitimately chattels of merchandise, but they were not the less important to the community; and when prepared and sold by gentlemen of the craft, were always more or less incentives to patronage.

John Elliot was a Quaker gentleman of kindly and winning manner, the popular apothecary of the neighborhood; at the same time making and preparing looking-glasses for the accommodation of the public in general. No. 60 knew him, and a goodly patronage knew *it*.

This No. 60 is a domain of some dignity, at least, for its dimensions. The house is of old style, but extensive in front and rear, the lot being about thirty-one feet front by over two hundred feet in depth, and widening in the rear from Gray's to Taylor's alley, having a front on each: the lot thus forming a **T**.

It is now the property of Wm. Geisse, who has lived in it and kept store as dealer in furs, looking-glass plates and German goods in general, as tenant and owner, for full thirty years.

Mr. Geisse, though of some seventy-six winters, is still fresh in the vigor of a green old age, active, acute and untiring in the business duties of the day—a good specimen of a German constitution.

In the day of the apothecary shop of No. 60, an M. D. flanked it at No. 62, and Doctor Samuel P. Griffiths was eminent here. Dr. Griffiths was amongst the early notables of his profession : 1802. Capt. John Collet occupied these premises in 1795.

John Dixon was an original manufacturer of mustard at No. 74. He was an English "Friend," and held popularity in his calling to his demise.

Jonathan Fell, the father of our cotemporary Franklin Fell, succeeded Mr. Dixon in the business, and connected with the manufactory of mustard that of chocolate and the grinding of spices. Mr. Fell was the competitor of my friend, Christian Hahn, of No. 104 North Front street.

Mr. Jonathan Fell was amongst the originators of the Lehigh Navigation Company, whose business was transacted at his store, No. 52, which, after his No. 74, he erected for manufacturing and general business purposes.

Of this Lehigh Navigation Company he was a member, trustee, or president, to the day of his death.

It may not be out of place to note here, that the first successful parlor grate for burning Lehigh coal was in the parlor of this Mr. Fell, which implement is now in the possession of his son, Franklin Fell.

Jonathan Fell died July 15, 1829, and was succeeded by his sons, C. & J. Fell, who afterward moved to No. 66, and thence to the south corner of Norris's alley and Front street.

This Fell establishment, originating with Dixon, dates from before the American Revolution, and hence was the oldest concern of the kind in Philadelphia.

Daniel King, eminent as a brass founder, was the industrious occupant of No. 76, where patronage and fortune smiled him into a successful issue of the reward of his labors; of which his son, Francis King of Arch street, is the happy beneficiary—a very excellent guardian of his father's legacies.

In 1795, and for many years after, there was no one more accustomed to the clang of the auction bell than John Connelly, whose No. 78 was heralded from day to day by the ding-dong of the important porter, as he paraded on the pave, calling attention to the public for a chance at the sale then and there to be made.

Mr. Connelly was one of the most prominent auctioneers of the day.

Our Manuel Eyre, of the firm of Eyre & Massey, married the daughter of this John Connelly, at the premises of the auction store, No. 80 South Front street, the residence of Mr. Connelly, about the year 1805, by the Rev. James Wilson, pastor of the First Presbyterian church.

This brings me to the merchandising mart of Samuel Coates, at No. 82, at the northwest corner of Front and Walnut streets.

This gentleman was a very estimable member of the Society of Friends, and was highly esteemed as the public benefactor in philanthropy, who, besides the *minutia* of his well-doing, was chosen and served as an efficient member of the Managers of the Pennsylvania Hospital for more than forty years. He died June 7th, 1830, in the eighty-second year of his age, and was ably and properly memorialized by our late valuable and highly respectable Roberts Vaux, which memorial was published in a public journal at the time, called "The Friend."

Were it not out of my line, I might here memorialize the

memorialist; and I am constrained to say, beyond my limits, that a more honest, public spirited, or more benevolent gentleman than Roberts Vaux, would be hard to find in Philadelphia, even now in the advancement of its age and the boasted march of improvement.

Roberts Vaux, under the firm of Vaux & Spangler, kept a wholesale dry goods store at No. 49 North Third street, about 1806.

CHAPTER XXIX.

Front street, East side—Walnut to Spruce—The Insurance Company of North America—Institution and Officers—John Vaughn—Edward Carrol—Isaac Wharton—David Lewis—Tribute to Francis Wharton—Odier & Bosquet—Lewis Glaises—Davy—Lewis—Custom-House, 1795—Its Officers—Owner of the Premises—Ross & Simpson—Lindo—Bringhurst—Henderson—Davy—Roberts—Doran—Buckley—Gilpins—Charles Wharton.

STRANGE as it may appear to the present generation, every step we take confirms the fact of these limits being the business, as well as the Court end of the town. The glare of Chestnut street was certainly not yet ignited, nor the grandeur of Walnut street even in embryo

The Insurance Company of North America was planted here, at the southeast corner of Front and Walnut, in 1795, the date of its institution, and gathered the neighboring merchants for its direction, which as matter of history, and recall of their manes, I give in detail.

Of this Company, Ebenezer Hazard was the Secretary; this was the sire of our cotemporaries, Samuel Hazard, our Pennsylvania Historian, and Erskine Hazard, a momentum of the Lehigh Navigation Company; and John Maxwell Nesbit was at the head—President of the following direction :—

Charles Petit,	Francis West
Thomas L. Moore,	John Craig,
Robert Ralston,	John Barclay,

12

Magnus Miller,	Michael Praegers,
John Ross,	John Leamy,
John Swanwick	Joseph Ball,
Walter Stewart,	John Blodget, Jr

Directory N. A. Insurance Co.

The details of mercantile life continue and show forth,

Firstly, at Nos. 109 and 111, our venerable and active John Vaughn, busily engaged in the importing and vending of wines; but Mr. Vaughn was more than this—he was a philanthropist of the first order—not of a smoldering spark of intentions, but a burning zeal to warm up the thrift and furtherance of others, to which end he devoted much of his time and money, and to the time of his death, was indefatigable in promoting the interests of strangers in a strange land.

Mr. Vaughn was a bachelor, but of estimable moral integrity, a man of good reputation for benevolence, steeped in the milk of human kindness.

He was a man of elastic energy, as I venture the evidence in the annexed portrait, but which an anecdote of his early life confirms.

His father objected to his entering into the risks of mercantile life, in the fear of failure; to which the son answered, "If I do fail, only give me a good oyster-knife, and I'll carve my way;" but he carved his way without it.

He was an Englishman by birth, prompt and fleet *au pied*. In winter, he wore a Scotch plaid cloak, carelessly thrown over his shoulders, the left side of the red collar jutting above the square of the other side—a memorable sign of John Vaughn, even afar off.

Mr. Vaughn died on the 20th of December, 1841, aged

eighty-five years; a decided loss to the poor, the widow, the fatherless, and the stranger in a strange land.*

Edward Carrol was a merchant, at No. 113, and Isaac Wharton and David Lewis were insurance brokers, at No. 115.

This Mr. Wharton was the father of our late eminent lawyer, Thomas I. Wharton, and the grandfather of our very useful citizen, Francis Wharton, Esq., son of Thomas I. Wharton, Esq., as above, whose services in our public schools, and untiring care and promotion of the youth, thus under his charge, cannot be negatived by time itself. Though happily still with us, and long may he remain, I owe him this testimony, and am right happy in the acknowledgment.

He is one of the most useful young men in the general cause of philanthropy, in our community.

But to my regular path. James Odier, and Bosquet & Brothers, French merchants, have claims to notice, at No. 117; and Lewis Glaisés, in like manner, at No. 119. But—

The United States planted her authority here, and divided the mercantile community right and left, until it plead "By your leave."

---

* Our distinguished mechanical genius, Mr. Samuel V. Merrick, of steam-engine notoriety, originated his business capacity in his counting-house, and under the patronage of Mr. Vaughan.   1815 to 1821.

Mr. Merrick, with his sons, now holds forth extensively under the incessant clang of the hammer and the rumbling roll of machinery, on Prime street below Fifth street, in full evidence of the growth and increase of popularity and prosperity.

Mr. Samuel V. Merrick has the credit of being the originator of the Gas-Works in Philadelphia, having erected the first Gas-Works in 1836, after his mission to England, in 1834, to investigate matters there, and mature them here, which he did as above, in 1836.

In 1795, the Custom-House for our district was located here, occupying seventy-six feet front, and through to Water street. The officers were in the second story, where every wight, anxious to pass the ordeal, was compelled to pay obeisance for the release of his ship-bound claims, and the furtherance of his speculative or more regular mercantile projects.

The officers of the institution, at that time, were,—

Sharp Delany, Collector.

Clement C. Brown, Deputy Collector.

Frederick Phile, Naval Officer.

William Macpherson, Surveyor.

John Graff, Weigher. Afterward Deputy Collector, 1805, and for many years; and Frederick Graff, Deputy Weigher, at the same time.

Thomas Pryor and William Milnor, Gaugers.

John Gill, Measurer, etc., etc.

In 1791, however, this centre of the revenue of our United States was located at the southeast corner of Second and Walnut streets, under the same direction.

The real estate occupied on Front street was the property of John Ross, who owned the breadth of seventy-six feet through to the wharf inclusive; and a part of the lower story of the Custom-House on Front street, was in the occupancy of Ross & Simpson, as *comptoir* and general place of business; all of which was the busy and important centre of the congregated mercantile community of Philadelphia, at that time.

The further details of mercantile life were in—

A. Lindo, a merchant, at No. 119.

James Bringhurst and Henry Henderson, both at No. 131.

William Davy and Joseph Roberts, shipping merchants, at No. 141.

Michael Doran, at No. 143.

William Buckley, at No. 147; and

Joshua Gilpin was a shipping merchant, at No. 149, in 1799; but subsequently was extensively engaged in the manufacture of paper, with his brother Thomas, under the firm of Joshua & Thomas Gilpin, whose paper-mills were located in, or near Wilmington, Delaware.

Joshua Gilpin was the father of our well-known barrister, Henry D. Gilpin, Esq., formerly Attorney-General of the United States under the administration of General Jackson.

In 1791, and long before and after, the late venerable Charles Wharton was actively engaged, first in the wholesale grocery trade, and afterward as an eminent shipping merchant and importer in the China trade.

He occupied the premises No. 153, through to Water street, where he probably originated his grocery business.

His residence was at No. 136 South Second street, near Spruce, a large and very superior mansion, having a flight of high and broad marble steps to its entrance; it was a noble structure of the day.

There were three of the same class adjoining each other; the No. 136 was occupied by Mr. Wharton; No. 138, a double front, by Robert Waln, and No. 140, by David Lewis.

Two of these structures still show up their dignity from the second story, the lower fronts having been modeled to business purposes; these are the former mansions of Robert Waln and David Lewis, of whom (Mr. Lewis), Mr. J. R. Mucherer, President of the Phœnix Mutual Insurance Co., is a son-in-law.

Mr. Wharton's house being about thirty feet front, has been transformed—two stores entirely obliterate its identity.

Mr. Wharton had attained to venerability even in my

younger day, to which his white capacious wig gave tone, as well as the measured gait that passed his tall and well-formed figure from his portal to the pave.

He died in the month of February, 1838, in the ninety-fifth year of his age.*

* He was in the full tide of business in the days of the American Revolution, seeing that the British burnt a fine ship for him, then nearly finished, on the stocks.

Rob.ᵀ Ralston

CHAPTER XXX.

THE mercantile community seemed to rally in this immediate compass, the east and west side of this square; and our
eminent merchant and valuable citizen, Robert Ralston, begins
the line at No. 90, in 1793; but afterward, in 1805, etc., he
was on the east side of Front, at No. 103, above Walnut; but
whether here or there, his business duties were seasoned with
the life of humanity, benevolence, and active Christian charity, and to do good unto all men, seemed ever to be his practical motto.

Miers Fisher, counselor at law, at No. 92, intercepted the
line, but not the notoriety of respectability, for Mr. Fisher
was prominent and popular in his profession, and of no small
moment in his social relations, as a member or adherent of
the Society of Friends.

David H. Cunningham and John M. Nesbit, trading under
the firm of Cunningham & Nesbit, were shipping merchants,
at Nos. 94 and 96; and James Stewart and James Barr, were
their neighbors, of No. 100, in the same occupation, under the
firm of Stewart & Barr.

Peter Blight, heretofore noted as an extensive shipping merchant and West India trader, of Ross's wharf, was resident here, at No. 102.

Abijah Dawes was at home here too, at No. 106, but abroad with his brother, Rumford Dawes, as copartners, shipping and importing from their counting-house and stores, east side of Water street below Market.

Here we have the root of an eminent, popular, and widely-known sea-captain, as well as of a well-known physician, for many years on the same spot.

Francis West, in company with his brother, John West, under the firm of Francis & John West, were popular merchants, at No. 108, 1791, and for many years after.

This Francis West was the sire of Capt. James West, who was long and favorably known as a commander in Cope's line of Liverpool ships, and afterward, in New York, as a popular commander of the finest steamship in the Liverpool trade.

Dr. Francis West succeeded his parents in the homestead of No. 108, and grew in his practice of medicine there; but his assiduity and fearless attention to the sufferers of the Cholera of 1832, contributed much to his fame and deserved popularity; and his disinterested liberality justly links him in the chain of benevolent men.

I must remark here, that as we near Dock street, the line of the latter being diagonal or scaunt, connected the Front street houses with the Dock street front; and hence we have Samuel R. Fisher, dealing in dry goods on Dock street, and retiring to his domicil on Front street, when his daily labors were over.

So, also Mordecai Lewis was largely engaged in the Calcutta, China, and European trade, popular and highly respectable, with his counting-house on Dock street, whilst his whereabouts was as well known at No. 112 South Front street, of course continuous with his counting-house. And—

Here again, we have a sire of *municipal* importance, and to Mordecai Lewis, the father of Joseph S. Lewis, prominent in our City Councils, and forward in the water-works improvements of Fairmount, and even now sculptured at Laurel Hill, belongs this memento.

Mordecai Lewis was also a prominent and active manager of the Pennsylvania Hospital, of which he was Treasurer from 1780 to 1799. His son, Joseph S. Lewis, succeeded him in that capacity, and served the institution till 1826. This Jos. S. Lewis was also President of the Schuylkill Navigation Company for many years, and there discharged its arduous duties to the entire satisfaction of the Company.

Mordecai Lewis, the father, was a respectable and efficient member of the Society of Friends.

William S. Sontag was prominent, at No. 114, as a shipping merchant in the West India trade, which, as heretofore shown, was as profitable as it was extensive, and the life of the " Yo, heave ho!" of the merry darkies, that rent the air with their vocal powers.

John Morton, of Morton's wharf, a dealer in flour there, retired here, at No. 116, from the laborious trusts and duties of the day, and after his *mercantile* pursuits was elected President of the Bank of North America, and filled his office successfully and creditably for many years. He was the third president in succession of that institution.

Here again, at No. 122, we have another root of a prominent character. "Purdon's Digest" is a work of notoriety, and popular at the bar of our Judiciary; and John Purdon, the father of the author of the "Digest," was not without *his* popularity as a dealer in dry goods here, sixty years ago.

Joseph Lowndes, though a prominent silversmith, was equally well known at No. 130, as an importer of China goods.

His neighbor of No. 132, was an M. D., represented in the person, skill, and services of Nathan Dorsey.

Lime was not exactly merchandise, yet it was desirable and important to the cementing of warehouses and other receptacles of safety. Lime-dealers, therefore, were a part of the corporation of mercantile stability, and in this commodity Samuel Richards was extensively engaged at No. 136.

This square closes with another *timeist:* and if John Mends was the minute-man on the other side, John McDowell was no less so here; for doubtless many a one stood before his regulator over the door to mark the dots of his dial, and perhaps haste to the point of his engagement.

CHAPTER XXXI.

Front street, East side—Spruce to Pine—Gurney & Smith—Daniel Smith—
His sons, Richard S., James S., Francis Gurney, Daniel S., Charles S., and
William S.—Moses Kempton—John Jones—J. O. Thompson.

WE come here to the drawbridge and its wide and busy
domains—still picturesque in my eye; but its details belong
not to me; but rather to the venerable Watson be the credit
for its details.

My business is to pass to the line of my general observation, and mark the spots of mercantile life as *they* marked
the history of early times.

Varied indeed was life here for a space; for after Andrew
Bankson and James Stuart's pharmaceutical mart at the southeast corner of Dock and Front streets, mercantile claims
were sunk, or intercepted, by a darksome row of small boarding-houses, even drying their necessary apparel at their front,
and claiming primitive simplicity and *nonchalance* as a prerogative.

But with due deference to the mercantile community, there
were others who contributed to the dignity of a neighborhood; and dark and sombre as the row before us, there was a
speck of light from the herald of an M. D. Doctor John
Porter, at No. 191, doubtless claimed and obtained the respectful attention due to his profession.

The reality of mercantile prowess, however, and the life
and spirit of its importance, gave tone to the square at No. 199.

Gurney & Smith were the active incumbents here in 1799, extensively engaged in the European and Calcutta trade, commercially interesting and important to the business community.*

As copartners they were popular—and favorably so; and as individuals, no less so. The one as General Francis Gurney, of whom, in turn, on the west side; the other as Daniel Smith, more in the immediate interests of the *protective* policy of the community, of which he before, had been a very prominent party.

He appears to have been a germ of political economy, and "insurance from life by fire" or water seems to have been a favorite scheme in him, from his counting-house to the elbow chair of indemnity for his fellow-citizens; for after his mercantile career he served successfully and satisfactorily as President of the Insurance Company of the State of Pennsylvania, at the northeast corner of Second and Dock streets, for many years.

His spirit, however, seems not to have departed with his mortal, seeing that sprouts of his acumen have started from the germ, and very respectable branches even now wave perpetuity to his manes.

It is not a little remarkable that of six sons, three of them herald the *memorabilia* of their father's fame; and even a *junior* branch fans the fame of his sire as an efficient and prominent item in the annals of insurance officers.

---

* As a link of history I note that the subsequent and celebrated—as well as our lamented Commodore Decatur—was clerk in the counting-house of Gurney & Smith, antecedent to his naval celebrity.

It is a remarkable fact coincident with his clerkship here, that he was sent by Gurney & Smith in pursuit of, and ordered the keel of the frigate "Philadelphia," which he afterward commanded.

In the first place, his sire, even in his mercantile life, after being one of the promoters of the Tree Insurance Company of Philadelphia, was an underwriter of policies at the Old Coffee House, where capitalists and men of courage were wont to resort and take a maritime risk; then president of an insurance office respectable and popular.

The vein courses in his son Francis Gurney Smith, and the chair of the Columbia Insurance Office is assigned to him for a season; then James S. Smith, Esq., aforetime a gentleman of the bar, gives dignity and character to the chair of the insurance office of "The Philadelphia Contributionship" for a term of seventeen years; whilst his brother, Richard S. Smith, is the efficient incumbent of the chair of "The Union Mutual Insurance Company:" and here I am met by the third generation of the same spirit.

James S. Smith, Esq., from the wear and waste of time, being now in his seventy-seventh year, has laid off his official mantle, and *his* son, James Somers Smith, has been endowed with its honors—an appointment, I am free to say, worthy of both sides of the question.

The whole family, as far as I have known them, have been prominent in usefulness, in public as well as social life, and gentlemen of winning suavity of manners; and to this day have lost nothing of their deserved popularity.

Francis Gurney Smith, the second son of our Daniel, has been a popular vestryman and warden of St. Peter's Church, Third and Pine street, for many years, an efficient protector of the rights and immunities of the temple and its grounds— a competitor of our worthy Moses Kempton, a very safe-guard of the same of Christ Church, Second near Market, who I name and memorialize here as a clerk of Jacob Clark of Water next below Arch—as a merchant in Front below

Arch in his hey-day, and as a useful member of society and especially so of the church of his adoption.

But to the link of the Messrs. Smiths. To Mr. Francis G. Smith may be ascribed the protectorate of the Musical Fund Society of Philadelphia, of which he has been treasurer, and it may be justly said, guardian, faithful to its trusts, from its beginning from nothing, to the hall that now heralds the fame of the Musical Fund Society.

Daniel Smith is a third son, once of the firm of Haven & Smiths, subjects of depression for a time; but, elastic and re-active, surmounts the hiatus of adversities and square accounts. Of this firm, Richard Smith was also one.

Our cotemporary Wm. S. Smith, for many years in the salt trade, and I believe successfully, and Charles S. Smith, for thirteen years treasurer of the Girard estate, bring me to a happy issue of that family of SMITHS.

This group of sons, successive in respectability and successful in their business relations, all living at this time, and ranging from sixty-one to seventy-six in years—being more than is commonly allotted to mortality and the changes and chances of human life—though foreign in detail to my legitimate purpose, is worthy of a line in history, and as such I venture the *interregnum* without fear, favor, or reward.

Mercantile notoriety appears to end here with Gurney & Smith, after noting John Jones, a merchant of No. 211, and Doctor Jacob Orier Thompson, who was doubtless an active spirit of the days of 1795 in this region.

CHAPTER XXXII.

Front street, West side—Spruce to Pine—Doctor Harris—J. W. Irwin—
George Plumstead—Archibald McCall—Francis Gurney—George Sibbald—
Dominick Joyce—Doctor James Mease—James Latimer—William Condy—
M. M. Carl—Condy Raquet—Chandler Price—Captain Toby.

THE southwest corner here was from time immemorial
a watchmaker's shop and residence; the most prominent
incumbent of which was for many years John Menzies, and
merchandising to Union street was limited. The line was tame
and rather sympathetic with the other side of the way, though
a better class of houses and occupants, gave tone to the
neighborhood. After Doctor Robert Harris, of No. 158, who
had his day and served his generation of 1795, mercantile
immunities seem to have been confined to John W. Irwin, of
No. 164, and George Plumstead and Archibald McCall, in the
East India trade, at No. 166.

The southwest corner of Front and Union even now sup-
ports a mansion of antique dignity, picturesque as well of its
times as of its early proprietor.

Here we have General Francis Gurney, of the firm of
Gurney & Smith, who in all probability located here in 1783,
as a business man, and continued here in his commercial
intercourse until Gurney & Smith bought, of Daniel Offley,*

---

* Daniel Offley was a prominent member and minister of the Society of
Friends. He died in 1793, a victim to his philanthropic energy and humane
sympathy in administering to the poor subjects of the yellow fever of that
year, and fell himself a sacrifice to their comforts and necessities.

his blacksmith's shop nearly opposite; and the *comptoir* of Gurney & Smith was a prominent mart of commercial interest in that square, where 1791 finds them.

Mr. Gurney, however, has claims to special notice.

First, we have him as a native boy of Montgomery County of 1738.

Secondly, a soldier in the British army in 1756, against the French and Indians on the frontiers of Canada.

Thirdly, we find him a marine in the British fleet against the French West India Islands.

Fourthly, in 1775, we find him a captain of infantry in the American army against the British; and in 1776 a lieutenant-colonel in the eleventh regiment of the Pennsylvania line.

He resigned his commission in the army from some disaffection at Valley Forge, but retained his public spirit in State and municipal services, more or less, during the thirty years of his mercantile labors, and retained his colonel's commission from 1786 to 1799, when he was promoted to the rank of brigadier-general, in which he was actively exercised against the Western Insurrection of 1794.

Mr. Gurney was thus a valuable and available citizen from the beginning to the very end of his life; and whether boy, soldier, captain, colonel, general, merchant, or retired citizen, we find him an active, energetic and important citizen of the United States, though unassuming and modest in all his relations in life, whether public or private.

His cotemporaries picture him as a remarkably fine-looking man, full six feet in height, well built, of dignified bearing, and distinguished in appearance.

He died May 25th, 1815, aged seventy-seven years.

His mansion of Union and Front street now belongs to his son-in-law, Charles A. Poulson, Esq., who lives next below—

of whom it is in my path to note that this relic could not be in better hands. Mr. Poulson being a very valuable antiquarian, and liberal in his expenditures for ancient landmarks of our city, of which his portfolio is vastly rich, and his notes and annotations replete with valuable statistics of our city.

George Sibbald, clerk in the Register's Office of the United States in 1793, presents himself at No. 170 as a shipping merchant, and Dominick Joyce joins in mercantile interest at No. 174.

No. 176 varied the mercantile chain here, in the medical emporium of Doctor James Mease, a link to elasticise longevity if possible. Doctor Mease was well-known, and doubtless popular in his day, of 1791.

He was the author of the "Picture of Philadelphia," published in 1811, esteemed as a valuable book of reference in *its* day.

Legal advice, though probably not so necessary then as now—still knots were to be untied and perhaps tied too—was to be had of James Latimer, Jr., at No. 178; and

William Condy, at No. 182, was always equal to the wants or the suggestions of clients.

This Mr. Condy was amongst the active originators of the Swedenborgian church, the first in Philadelphia, built at the southeast corner of Twelfth and George streets, of which Maskil M. Carl was the pastor, about A. D. 1820; in which, right or wrong, Mr. Condy was faithful to his profession, and Mr. Carl a devoted pioneer in the ministry of that denomination.

As matter of history, I take occasion to note, as the edifice has given way long since to domestic requirements, that it was a square building, having a dome, of limited area in the

13

interior, and an organ gallery immediately over the pulpit at the east end of the church.

Our Mr. Wm. Condy and his nephew, Condy Raquet, were efficient members of the Society; and our old friend, Daniel Thunn, a happy believer in the views of Emmanuel Sweden-borg.

Chandler Price, after the firm of Morgan & Price, of No. 170 North Front street in 1779, was here at No. 214 in 1802

He was long and favorably known as a pioneer in the New Orleans trade, when it first became a part of our Union, and established a line of packets to that port. Our venerable Captain Simon Toby commanded one of ships, the "Ohio," for several years in that trade, and was highly esteemed for his urbanity, prudence and success.

After his—Captain Toby's—retirement, he was the President of the Insurance Company of the State of Pennsylvania, which office he filled very acceptably to his constituents for many years.

He is still living, being upward of eighty years of age.

CHAPTER XXXIII.

Front street—East side—Pine to South—Ignatius Paillard—Francis Coppinger—Levinus Clarkson—Jones & Clark—Capt. William Jones—Samuel Clark—John Swanwick—Roe Brumard—Joseph Read—S. & W. Keith—Derrick Peterson—Robert Bridges—Henry Mitchel—Augustine & John Bousquet, 1799—Peter Bousquet, 1805.

THE atmosphere of mercantile life spread onward, and the corner here marked its continuance.

Ignatius Paillard set this corner as a mercantile mart, and Francis Coppinger followed suit next below, at No. 221; and again, Levinus Clarkson strengthened the line of shipping merchants here, but the firm of Jones & Clark, at No. 225, in 1800, seems to have had more in them than the ordinary run of mercantile prowess; the firm, however, built and owned many vessels to carry out their East India, Canton, and European trade.

Wm. Jones had been a sea-captain himself, and had some genius in draughting and constructing vessels to meet the caprice of old Neptune; and hence, probably, in 1812, Mr. Madison, our President of the United States, chose him for Secretary of the Navy, in which, after a service of some three or four years, he was appointed the first President of the Bank of the United States, of 1816.

After this we find him the Secretary of the American Fire Insurance Company, at No. 101 Chestnut street; and again we have him Collector of the Port of Philadelphia, where he also remembered his former business associate, and no doubt, influenced the appointment of Samuel Clark as naval officer. Jones & Clark had, therefore, *made* service in mercantile life, *seen* service in maritime risks, and *done* service to the general government of the United States.

John Swanwick, heretofore noted, was resident at No. 237, but was continuous in presence and profession through to Penn street, where the changes and chances of mercantile life, either lit up or beclouded his path as common to all men.

Roe Brumand, at 247, and Josph Read, at 271, contributed to the mercantile life of 1795, in the square; and Samuel & William Keith counted the cost of their many ships, and averaged the profits of freight or charter as incentive or tact suggested: for they were shipping merchants as well as owners of many vessels, 1795, and many years afterward.

In 1823, Samuel Keith had withdrawn from the immediate risks of merchandising, and became supervisor of the risks of others, as President of the Delaware Insurance Company.

Intermediately in this quarter at No. 223, Derrick Peterson was resident; whilst as active lumber merchant he was enclosed in lumber, timber and boards below Almond street; withal, he was an important item of his day there.

So also was Robert Bridges, of No. 259, *the* sailmaker of the day, and the *baas* of James Forten, set forth in the proper place of his hey-day; and again, Henry Mitchell, a ropemaker, of 261, as important to Bridges as he was to Captain McFadden of 275, who kept him alive to their importance.

Augustine & John Bousquet were prominent and popular French merchants at No. 267, a highly-respectable mercantile house of 1799, long before and after. But *Peter* Bousquet, our presen venerable fellow-citizen, came over from France in 1805, and continued the respectability of the house for many years.

Mr. Peter Bousquet is therefore still amongst us, a pleasing specimen of a retired merchant, aud a happy issue of the sere and yellow leaf of human nature, endowed with a rubicund countenance and the beau ideal of a *gentilhomme à son vise.*

CHAPTER XXXIV.

Front street—West side—Pine to South—George B. Dawson—J. & W. Lynch
—Lewis Clapier—Budaraque—John Latour—J. C. Stocker—John Morton
—John Barclay—Philip Kelly—Samuel Reid—James Traquair.

ON this side of the square the mercantile community di-
minished, and the principal life of merchandising seems to
have been vested in George B. Dawson, of No. 184, and John
& Wm. Lynch, of No. 186; but the most prominent spirit of
the time, 1802, was the popular Lewis Clapier, an extensive
shipping merchant, resident next below the corner of Lombard
street—counting-house on Lombard street.

Mr. Clapier was in the French trade, and with his chief
clerk, Mr. Budaraque, held commercial counsel with his brother
in Marseilles; but besides this his commercial interest connected him with China, East India, Havanna, Vera Cruz, etc.,
1802 to 1826 and after. He owned many ships, all paying their
way profitably. His Mr. Budaraque was an important fixture
of his *comptoir*, an efficient aid in his pursuits. He was, however, an inveterate smoker, seldom without a cigar—at reading, writing or ciphering, a cigar! indeed, it was said of him,
that he could smoke two at the same time: to wit, one in each
corner of his mouth.

I cannot pass this corner without a respectful notice of
John Latour, celebrated, if for nothing else, as the importer
and very popular vendor of salad, or sweet oil.

He was a merchant in the French trade at No. 8 Lombard

street, but subsequently located on the east side of Front street, nearly opposite to Lombard street; but whether here or there, salad oil memorializes him to this day.

He dates there at and before 1807.

But other business life animated the scenes of this compass.

John Clement Stocker filled the aldermanic chair of No. 188 South Front street, in 1795, where he doubtless kept the wayward in check by admonition or commitment; whilst his neighbor, Captain John Morton, relieved him from time to time from the onus by the shipment of the unwary and untoward disturbers of the peace.

Mr. Stocker was a prominent member of the community, and active and successful in business life.

His exports to, and imports from China told well to his treasury and furthered his liberal disposition, for his reputation was that of a helpful friend in need. As a merchant he was popular, and his memorabilia is still unscathed by time; whilst as a public man, the records of the Insurance Company of the State of Pennsylvania, as well as those of the *Bank* of Pennsylvania, bear testimony of his services there for many years.

He was a man of wealth, with an open hand and a sympathetic heart.

Of the several first-class three-story brick houses in this region, No. 216 was the residence of John Barclay, Esq., one of the early presidents of the Bank of Pennsylvania, and No. 218 that of Philip Reily, another merchant of the day.

Samuel Reid, too, had his day as merchant at 234: and thus far closes the mercantile array.

This same No. 234 was aforetime the dot and line of James Traquair, a spirited and progressive stone-cutter, who came over from Greenock in 1784.

Mr. Traquair afterward built up the southeast corner of Tenth and Market streets, with lower marble front, had his yard on the rear, and put up a marble pigeon-box in the rear of his dwelling—the first of the kind in Philadelphia. He bought much of the remains of Morris's Folly, and incorporated some of it in his new building, which building was remarkable in its day and location.

We trace here the father of the late Adam Traquair, City Commissioner, and the grandfather of James Traquair, now one of the firm of Morris L. Hallowell & Co.. silk merchants of No. 333 Market street.

CHAPTER XXXV.—CONCLUSION.

Review and General Remarks.

HAVING concluded my search and research, some apology may be due for the apparent incongruities of my details:

My History purports to be of the mercantile community of some fifty to seventy years ago; and so in fact it is—but perhaps, in form, a mixture; and hence it behooves me to defend myself for my course, and satisfy the reader for the shades of the picture.

To write a mere detail of merchants, as they stood side by side—however historical—would be but a meagre relation of facts, without a tint of the variety that lights the course and gives color to what else would be a monotony.

Moreover, I could not prosecute my line of march without touching the appendages,—the *olden time* being the basis of my history. Hence the great and the small meet *en passant.*

Every block had its variety, and reminiscence seemed to urge its claims; but these very *claims* light up the picture, and show up men, manners and things of the past, and take their place on the page of history.

But the mercantile community is in no way disparaged by the course.

In regard to the merchants themselves, and their respective locations, they are as existent at the time specified.

It may, however, be objected that this, that, or the other

was here or there located; truly so, but not within my compass of time. I might and I could have given a succession to the various locations; but my original plan forbade the extension, and expediency frowned at an undue volume.

In traversing the Wharves from north to south, I offer their identity, at and about the time, as graphic; seeing that memory is confirmed not only by like collateral testimony, but by the artistic evidence of drafts of their various features, made more than fifty years ago.

Again, the mercantile community that gave life to scenes and scenes to active life, is given as it then was; and may show up to "Young America" the wit, the wisdom, the prudence, the prowess of its forefathers.

History is an important tome to the world itself, else, whence the knowledge of any thing of the past? Is it to pass into the mystic clouds of oblivion, or be shut up in the *bosom* of antiquity? Is it to cease with its breath, and pass as though it ne'er had been? I trow not.

Philadelphia has not been a mere speck in the commercial horizon—not a mere dot on the map of geographical details. She had a proud bearing on the world of commerce; her port was courted, caressed, and embraced by almost every nation, and was the very bosom of the nurture of commerce. Her merchants were men of courage and enterprise; nor were their operations merely speculative: their results, generally, were unmistakable evidences of well-digested plans and sound judgment.

"Young America" presses onward, unmindful of the past, and, sad to say, untutored by the experience of her fathers; she forgets or repudiates the intellectual wealth of her ancestors, and seems proud of the golden bowl of her newly-dis tilled wisdom; her yesterday is her starting point, and her to-morrow the consummation of her projects.

Not so, the fathers of the olden time—*they* gathered wisdom as bees gather honey: and *their* hives were redolent of the sight and the savor of well-digested architectural genius, giving tone, dignity, and character to the field of their labors.

Shall the early dignity of Philadelphia be evaporated in the fog of impetuous ambition, and our posterity bow the knee or shrink before a sister whose robes and flounces are the trimmings of fortuity? We, the remnant of the olden time, say, No! We look back upon the proud bearing of our port, and say, No! We claim *perpetuity* to the manes of our early merchants; we fondle with the *bouquet* of their gathering, and pass it to posterity as a rich relic of the hey-day of Philadelphia, and present it to our rival, in token of remembrance of our former superiority.

The mercantile community, as here portrayed, has claims worthy of the pages of history; and there let them be planted, and thence grow upon the mind, memory, and understanding of "Young America," until it chasten her haste, guide her footsteps, and qualify her wisdom.

In all this, we would not shade the glory of our sister city, but rather, as a member of our confederacy, congratulate her upon the bountiful sunshine of her prosperity; but we cannot forego the fact, that *nature* has been her *alma mater*, and *art* the panderer to her thrift, and that the jointure has built her up a mighty city—whilst the glory of Philadelphia was rayed by the acumen, the courage, and the perseverance of our fathers, and warmed to the dignity due to a commercial port, independent of the natural solicitations of our neighbour.

Neither would we detract from our mercantile community

of the present day—*they* live and act under a different *regime;* the influence of "Young America" elasticises their atmosphere, and spurs the heel at the expense of the head: lighting their path merely from the *tips* of the radii without consulting the brow of their source.

We have good men and true amongst us, who, whilst some are estimable representatives of their ancestors, and would hand down to posterity the mercantile dignity of their fathers, others, not of the same spirit, suffer loss by a disregard of the more dignified platform of characteristic merchandising, and sink their skill in the *minimum,* instead of raising it to the *maximum* of mercantile dignity.

The contrast between the present and the past, in regard to the commercial enterprise of Philadelphia's merchants, is certainly very severe; and we of the senior class of her sons, cannot but lament and even weep over causes and effects. And although we are about to uncoil our mortal cordage, we are none the less sensitive of any disparagement of our foster home—nay, even more, our *amour patri* centres in our homestead, and our proneness to review and fondle with the things of our youth becomes a text for our mental meanderings.

Hence then a concentration of reflection, a gathering of happy recollections, and the incidental review that presses thought to speech, and speech to the intelligence that profits by the past, and shapes or qualifies the future.

With all this, I abjure the charge or suspicion of a *fancy* sketch, or a subterfuge of heavy time—that ingredient in human life is not mine—but I cannot deny my ardent love for ruminating over the green fields of my youth, rejuvenating in the pastures of reminiscence, and feeding upon the herbs that revive the spirits of wasting life as it wanes and diminishes on the inclined plane of mortality.

A picture of the past is ever and anon grateful to the eye of a senior. So to your author; and little in the world more to his taste, than the busy life that glistened his eye as he roved in the precinct that lit up the life of his city, and gave tone from its centre to the circumference of its influence.

The picture is before you, and, to the best of my knowledge and belief, a truthful delineation.

If, in some of my details, I have been more extensive than in others, they have been given as samples only of the prowess of the merchants of the day; nothing eulogistic whatever is intended—there was a difference truly, but no disparagement; but the whole together was a crown of glory to the community of our city.

Times have changed, and circumstances have altered cases; our men and their manners are gone; very few of the list remain. We hail the present—we salute the memory of the past; and whilst our respectful tribute to their manes be their epitaph, let the *bouquet* of their career be a refreshing savor of the commercial dignity, the mercantile wealth, and the well deserved fame of Philadelphia and her merchants, as constituted fifty to seventy years ago!

APPENDIX.

Jonathan Ludlow
7mo 26ᵗʰ 1848

APPENDIX.

IF a Preface is necessary to inform the kindly patron of the
intent and meaning of an author, and an Introduction a pre-
lude to a prefatory apology for what he *has* done, a Note
en finale for what he has *not* done may be no less important,
at least for his own benefit, to clear his skirts as he retires
from his historical pursuit to the charm of freedom and rest
from his labors, and passes his work to the critique of the
historian, or the fastidiousness of the world's literati.

In a retrospect of fifty to even eighty years perspective,
memory must be severely taxed, and collateral testimony no
less tested, to avert the plea of "errors and omissions ex-
cepted"; and here, although I flatter myself the former are
"few and far between," the latter rise up in judgment against
me, and call for their share of historical identity. And
although I may still be at fault, they that present themselves
have claims, and must be brought forth to resume their posi-
tions in the mercantile life that gave tone to the early commercial prosperity of Philadelphia and her cheerful and
lucrative port.

14 (209)

Amongst the missing in the body of the work, Jonathan Leedom was not the least of the mercantile spirits of his day, 1805 and onward.

He was located at No. 182, on the east side of Front street, above Pine street—store through to Water street.

He was a shipping merchant in good standing, engaged in the Liverpool trade, and at the same time and in the same place kept a wholesale iron store for many years after he ceased to be a shipowner, even until the time of his death: to wit, December 17, 1848, being then in his seventy-fourth year. He was born in Cheltenham, Bucks County. Mr. Leedom was a member of the Society of Friends, and was highly esteemed for his correct deportment.

Here again a respectful recognition of Benjamin Jones, Jun., is due.

Mr. Jones had his store and counting-house in the same building with Mr. Leedom. He, too, was a shipping merchant, engaged in the Liverpool and Bordeaux trade; a man highly esteemed for his integrity in all his business transactions.

About the year 1836 he was chosen by our City Councils treasurer of the Girard trust, which office he held for several years.

The memory of this gentleman links with that of the late venerable Joseph Sims, in whose counting-house he was brought up, was with him in the days of his prosperity, and served him and his creditors as assignee of his estate in the day of his adversity.

Robert Oakley, although not in this connection of *localie*, was a shipping merchant and shipowner, of and about 1802; he was also an occasional importer of Canton goods; his counting-house was No. 22 Dock street—his shipping, of course, contributed to the commercial life of the times.

John Craig, no less important to commercial life, had his counting-house at No. 12 Dock street in 1799.

He was a shipping merchant of high standing, largely engaged in the Vera Cruz trade, particularly in the importation of large quantities of specie (Spanish dollars) from Mexico. Mr. Craig prospered to vast possessions.

He was the father-in-law of the late Nicholas Biddle, of whom I cannot forego the opportunity to say that he, Nicholas Biddle, was a gentleman, a scholar, and a man of fine literary attainments; although unfortunate in misplaced popularity, where he might well have cried "Save me from my friends," political and social, if weighed in the balance would have been found more sinned against than sinning.

George Armroyd was part and parcel of the commercial life of 1802, being in the St. Croix trade, an extensive importer of the finest sugar from that quarter—a house in good standing. His counting-house was at 109 South Water street, in 1802; but in 1805 was at No. 125 South Front street.

John Coulter was another enterprising spirit of the early time. He was a shipping merchant of No. 210 South Water street, and was extensively engaged in the European and West India trade—a large importer and exporter of goods, wares, and merchandise.

He was noted for industry, perseverance, and personal application to business, and was not afraid of work, and was prominent in commercial life from 1802 and onward. Mr. Coulter was also, at one period, a Director of the Bank of the United States of 1816.

After his retirement from the busy scenes and labors of merchandising, he retired to his farm near Germantown, and there, too, finished his course on the 16th day of December, 1857, at the very ripe old age of nearly eighty-five years.

The celebrated firm of Smith & Ridgway has been noticed in its proper place; but subsequently, 1803, their apprentice and clerk became a "Co." to the firm: Samuel W. Jones being this junior partner.

After the retirement of Mr. Ridgway, Mr. Jones was continued as the partner of James Smith, under the firm of James Smith & Co., 1806, at No. 154 North Front street, and was an active and efficient spirit of the concern, helping it, doubtless, to a successful issue.

They transacted a large and lucrative business, sending their vessels to foreign ports, particularly to Antwerp, where their old partner, Mr. Ridgway, had established himself as a merchant, acting also at the same time as American consul.

Mr. Jones is yet our cotemporary; who, although even now in his seventy-ninth year, shows up the force of his early day in the firmness and activity of his foot, and the clearness of a mind unclouded and unimpared by time; and I greatly fear that very few of our rising generation will attain to such a desert and just tribute, due to him and many more of the olden time.

In reference to this location, I note further that there were four first-class three-story brick houses on this lot, running south from Key's alley about eighty feet, of which Jacob Ridgway occupied the corner of Key's alley as No. 160; James Smith, his partner, next below, No. 158; George W. Morgan, No. 156, afterward of Arch street below Tenth; and Smith, Ridgway & Co. had their counting-house at No. 154—all of which were destroyed in the conflagration of that quarter in 1850.

Alexander J. Derbyshire still perpetuates the memory of Timothy Paxson, whom he served as apprentice and clerk, and even now succeeds him in the same business and on the *same spot*, upon which he erected an extensive store, with very handsome and capacious counting-house accommodations.

To return to the olden time, however. Memory challenges an active and notorious spirit of commercial and *maritime* life.

CAPTAIN DAVID MOFFAT, after a term of some years in mercantile pursuits,—first, in 1805, located at No. 28 Walnut street, and afterward, in connection with Thomas Burke and James Caldwell of No. 3 South Wharves, in the Spanish trade—distinguished himself greatly in the war with Great Britain in 1812, as a terror to the merchantmen of the enemy.

He commanded the fleetest privateers out of the United States, and scoured the coast of Great Britain to its great annoyance and loss, by his frequent captures of her merchant ships.

He was a man of indomitable courage and untiring perseverance, and was renowned for his skill and success and generosity as a privateersman.

After his privateering, CAPT. MOFFAT was Master Warden of the port of Philadelphia for many years in succession, appointed by various Governors of the State of Pennsylvania, which office he held until his decease in Philadelphia, on the 1st of May, 1838, at an advanced age.

But it was not *all* commerce that built up Philadelphia: there were active adventurers from the counting-house on the wharf to the environs of the city, compassed by post and rail fences.

Thomas Pratt, in the freshness of his youth, struck from the desk to the open commons to invest inactive capital and act a pioneer in improvements of our city.

In 1805 he took up the southwest corner of Eleventh and

Chestnut streets, from Samuel W. Fisher, then guarded by
a post-and-rail fence, at six dollars ground-rent per foot for
sixty feet on Chestnut street by two hundred and thirty-five
feet to George street, and built three three-story brick houses
on Chestnut street and seven on Eleventh street—this was
entirely out of town at that time. He tells me there were but
two brick houses between that and the Schuylkill, and they
were inside of the southwest corner of Twelfth and Chestnut
streets; they stood back considerably from the line and were
enclosed by a board fence.

Again in 1808, the embargo crippling our commerce, his
enterprise sought vent in another purchase of fifty feet of
ground opposite the Academy of Fine Arts, from Thomas
Biddle, also at six dollars per foot ground-rent, the lot also
two hundred and thirty-five feet to George street; here he
erected two large mansions of twenty-five feet each, which
he afterward sold, one to the celebrated Commodore Truxton,
and the other to our late fellow-citizen, Thomas Hale, of the
popular firm of McEwen, Hale & Davidson, of Dock street,
brokers.

Two years after the above purchase, the adjoining lots
westward, were sold at fifteen dollars per foot ground-rent.

Mr. Pratt is even yet in the comfortable enjoyment of a
green old age, being of sound mind, memory and understanding, taking his daily walk *nonchalant* of any *extraordinary* waste of time's efforts, although in his eighty-seventh
year.

The firm of Yorke & Lippincott, auctioneers, has been
noticed in its proper place; but as it was the most popular
concern of the day, it may not be uninteresting to memorialize its origin and succession.

Peter Benson was what was then, 1797, called a Vendue Master, and held forth at No. 74 South Third street.

In 1799 he associated with him Samuel Yorke, who had been brought up in the business by Richard Footman, auctioneer, at No. 65 South Front street in 1793, and the firm in 1799 was Benson & Yorke, at No. 39 North Front street.

Mr. Benson retired, and Samuel Yorke conducted the business alone, at No. 41 North Front street, 1802. In 1805 Joshua Lippincott was the partner of Mr. Yorke; and for several years the firm was Yorke & Lippincott, at No. 51 North Front street.

The decease of Mr. Yorke gave place to John Humes, and Humes & Lippincott continued the business as above. Mr Humes retired, and the firm changed to Joshua & William Lippincott, by the association of William, the brother of Joshua. This firm was succeeded by Lippincott & Richards —Benjamin W. Richards, the new associate, being the son-in-law of Joshua Lippincott: and here ends that succession. Mr. Richards afterward pursued the business in Front near Chestnut, in company with Joseph Bispham, under the firm of Richards & Bispham, where in time the succession in that occupation ceased, and Benjaman W. Richards was subsequently elected Mayor of the city—a very gentlemanly municipal magistrate.

The above business firms were in good standing from first to last, eminent in business tact, and stood most prominent in popularity and patronage as auctioneers.

In the succession of the Treasuryship of the Pennsylvania Hospital, I omitted the last link of the chain in its proper place. And an unbroken descent of an important trust in the same family, being of no common occurrence, I take occasion here to repeat the fact, and add the link—

Mordecai Lewis, Treasurer, - - -   1780 to 1799, 19 years.
Joseph S. Lewis,   "   - - -   1799 to 1826, 27   "
Samuel M. Lewis,   "   - - -   1826 to 1841, 15   "
John T. Lewis,   "   the grand-
    son of Mordecai, and present in-
    cumbent,   -   -   -   -   1841 to 1859, 18   "

Shows a succession of *seventy-nine years* in the direct line of the same family!

As further matter of history I add, that the above Mordecai Lewis was, in his early day, the partner of the celebrated William Bingham, whose mansion and open grounds once beautified the neighborhood of Third and Spruce, now transformed and transferred to the business world by Joseph Harrison, Jun., and others.

PHILADELPHIA:
STEREOTYPED BY GEORGE CHARLES,
PRINTED BY KING & BAIRD,
607 SANSOM STREET.

PREFIX TO THE SUBSCRIPTION LIST.

It was a custom of the olden time to append to almost every Literary or Historical work, "The Names of Subscribers." Fashion or fancy, however, seems to have plead the custom from its usual page, and left the patron untold of liberality, and even to sleep in the vacuum of oblivion.

With a truce to the idea, my emotions seem to forbid the omission, seeing that a full measure of gratitude is due to the kindly recognition of my efforts, and the highly respectable patronage that ensued.

Unwilling to be derelict of grateful considerations, I cannot pass the page that offers its services to perpetuate the kindly regard to an humble author, and the author's grateful return for the grant to his plea.

But, whilst in doing this, an apology will be due to those who do not appear—and this because their names have not been returned in time for this issue—another may be important to many whose retiring modesty would as willingly have shrunk from the notoriety of a subscribtion list.

Let the one however be assured that my thanks are no less rife in the omission, and the other be sought to sink their demurrer in the unfeigned assurance of unintentional offense of a GRATEFUL AUTHOR!

(217)

SUBSCRIPTION LIST.

Abbott, George.
Adams' Express.
Allen, T. W.
Allinson, William.
Anderson, William V.
Anspach, J., Jr.
Ashhurst, Richard.
Ashhurst, John.
Ash, J. P.
Ashley & Sharpe.
Audenried, Lewis.

Backus, F. R.
Bacon, Alexander.
Bacon, Franklin.
Bacon, J. K.
Badger, William.
Baker, Abraham.
Baker, Alfred H.
Baker, Charles H.
Baker, Isaac F.
Bancker, Charles N.
Barclay, A. C.
Barcroft, S. B.
Baumgardner, J. G.
Beck, Henry Paul.
Beck, James N.
Bell, John.
Benner, H. L. .8
Biddle, Edward C.
Biddle, William.
Binns, John.
Bishop, Charles F.
Bohlen, John.
Boller, Henry J.

Bond, S. Montgomery.
Boric, C. & H.
Bousquet, Peter.
Bradford, William.
Bradford, B. Rush.
Brown, David S.
Browne, Benneville.
Brooke, Stephen H.
Burton, John.
Bussier, Joseph B.
Bute, Charles L.
Butcher, John.
Butler, William S.

Campbell, John H., Esq.
Carrigan, C. W.
Carver, Samuel.
Carstairs, James.
Carson, H. L.
Carson, J., M.D.
Cetti, A. C.
Chamecen, U.
Cheyney, Charles H.
Chester, Lewis.
Christ, Jay & Hess.
Christian, S. J.
Chur, A. T.
Clark, Edward L.
Clark, Joseph.
Claghorn, John W.
Claghorn, James L.
Claghorn, William C.
Claghorn & Fryer.
Clothier, J. H.
Coates, Benjamin.

(218)

Coffin, Lewis.
Connarroe, George M.
Conrad, Harry.
Cooper, C. Campbell, M.D.
Cooper, Parham & Work.
Cook, Jay.
Cooley, A. B.
Cope, F. R.
Cornelius, Robert.
Coulter, S.
Craig, William.
Cresson, Charles M.
Cresson, John C.
Cresson, William P.
Cregar, P. A.
Crissy, James.
Cross, Edward H.
Cross, Michael H.
Curran, Lewis, M.D.
Cuyler, Theodore, Esq.

Da Costa, John C.
Dale, Edward C.
Dammond Raymond.
Darrach, William, M.D.
Darrach, Thomas B.
Darley, W. H. W.
Darling, John A.
Davis, Daniel S.
Dawson, T. Russel,
Dawson, Mordecai L.
Day, G. W.
De Brot, John.
Degrange, Stephen A.
Denckla, A. H.
Denckla, H. Albert.
Denckla, F. W.
Denckla, Paul.
Denckla, C. Paul.
Dennison, David W.
Dennison, J. Harry.
Derbyshire, Alex. J.
De Schweinitz, Rev. Ed. A.
Ditzler, William U.
Doll, George, & Co.
Drexel, A. J.
Dreer, F. W.
Dulles & Cope.
Dundas, James, Esq.

Dutilh, Charles.

Earp, Thomas.
Earp, Theodore.
Elliot, Isaac.
Elliott, James.
Esler, George, Jr.
Esler, L. H.
Evans, Thomas W.
Evans, James R.
Everly, William A.

Fell, Franklin.
Fenimore, J. L.
Ferguson, Bryant.
Fitler, A.
Fling, William B.
Flood, Samuel F.
Folwell, T. G.
Fontanges, P. F.
Ford, John M.
Fraley, F.
Franciscus, A. H.
Fry, John A.
Fryer, George.
Fuller, Oliver.
Furness, Brinley & Co.

Gaillard, Edward, Jr.
Gans, Leiberman & Co.
Gaw, Alexander G.
Gaw, Henry L.
Geisse, William & Sons.
Gerhart, Isaac.
Getze, J. A.
Gibbons & Cantadore.
Gibbons, James S.
Gilbert, Henry R.
Gillespie, Thomas L.
Gillespie, William.
Godley, Henry.
Godley, Jesse.
Godfrey, Benjamin G.
Goff, J. W.
Goodwin, Thomas F.
Gordon, James.
Gould, J. E.
Gratz, Edward.
Grant, Samuel.

Greiner & Harkness.
Grigg, John.
Griffiths, Mary.
Gross, George J.
Guillou, Rene.
Guliger, William.

Haguer, Charles V.
Hallowell, Joshua L.
Hallowell, William P.
Hamm, P. E.
Hand, Thomas C.
Hand, James C.
Hart, William H.
Harrison, Joseph.
Hazard, Erskine.
Helffenstein, Emanuel.
Hemphil, John.
Henry, Alexander, Esq.
Hensel, Daniel.
Henderson, George A.
Herline, Edward.
Heyl, Theodore C.
Heiskel, Wm. B., Esq.
Hill, Marshall.
Hildeburn, J. H.
Hockley, John.
Homer, Benjamin, Jr.
Hopper, Edward, Esq.
Horner, Benjamin C.
Horstman, Sigmund.
Horstman, W. J.
Hovey, Franklin S.
Howell, H. C.
Hutchinson, E. R.
Hutchins, Mason.

Jacobsen, Henry G., Esq., Balt.
Jackson, Charles C.
Janney, S. M.
Jayne, E. C.
Jeanes, Thomas.
Jeanes, J. T. & S.
Johnson, R. S.
Johnes, George W.
Jones, Joseph.
Jones, Samuel W.
Jordan, Francis.
Jordan, John.

Justice, George M.

Keene, James W.
Keller, J. B.
Kemper, J. L. A
Kent, William C.
Kern, Horatio G.
Kibbin, J. W.
Kimber, Thomas, Jr.
King, D. Rodney.
King, Francis.
Kirkham, William.
Kline, J. N.
Krug, F. V. & Co.

Lancaster, J. B.
Latimer, Thomas, Esq.
Lawson, John L.
Lee, R. M., Esq.
Lee, J.
Leedom, B. J.
Lehman, E. W.
Leiper, Wm. J.
Lennig, C. & F.
Leslie, C. M.
Levy, L. J. & Co.
Lewis, Edwin N.
Lewis, Henry, Jr.
Lewis, Joseph W.
Lewis, John T.
Lewis, Saunders.
Lewis, W. D., Esq.
Lewis, Walter H.
Lex, Charles E., Esq.
Lex, Charles F.
Link, John.
Lippincott, J. B. & Co.
Littel S., M.D.
Littel, A. R.
Livezy, John.
Lodge, Jonathan.
Lueders, Thomas L.

Maenel & Scheppler.
Magee, James.
Marston, John, Capt. U. S. N.
Martin, A.
Martin, James.
Mason, James.

Masson, Charles H.
Massey, Charles, Jr.
Massey, R. V.
Mann, William.
Maxfield, Joseph.
Mellizet, F. W.
Merrick, S. V.
Messchert, M. H.
Miller, William.
Mitcheson, M. J., Esq.
Mooney, Amos M.
Morrison, Mrs. A. D.
Morrel, Schroeder & Fergnson.
Morrel & Stokes.
Morrel, Thomas.
Moss, A. A.
Moss, E. L.
Moss, Eli T.
Moss, Joseph L.
Moss, Lucien.
Musser, William.
Myers, John B.

McAllister, John.
McAllister, John A.
McAllister, Thomas H.
McCrea, John.
McKibbon, W. C.

Needles, Caleb H.
Needles, E. M.
Needles, J. A.
Needles, William N.
Newbold, William H.
Newell, William.
Newland, Edward.
Norris Thaddeus.

Ogden, Charles J.
O'Neal, John L.

Page, Washington.
Parrish, Dillwyn.
Parrish, George.
Parker, John H.
Patterson, Joseph.
Patterson, Jonathan.
Patterson, Gen. Robert.
Peabody, Edward G.

Pearson, Davis.
Pennock, Abraham L.
Patterson, Thomas R.
Petit, Edgar E.
Philler, George, Jr.
Phillips, B.
Phillips & Brother.
Potter, Alfred R.
Poulson, Charles A.
Price, Eli K., Esq.
Price, Joseph.
Price, Joseph N.
Price, J. M. P.
Price, Richard.
Price, Richard, Jr.
Price, J. Sergeant, Esq.
Price, Stephen S.
Purves, Wm.

Randall, A. L.
Randall, J. H., Esq.
Rasin, Warner M.
Rednor, Jos.
Rednor, Lewis H.
Reed & Co.
Reed, R. S.
Reed, Wm. J.
Rehn, Caspar L.
Rehn, Wm. L.
Reigel, Jacob.
Reneker, John.
Repplier, John G.
Rice, John.
Richards, Benj. W.
Richardson, Charles.
Richardson, Richard.
Ritchie, Craig D., Esq.
Ritter, Benj. J.
Ritter, Miss Mary.
Roberts, David.
Roberts, Edward.
Robinson, A. S.
Robinson, Abraham.
Robinson, Thos. A.
Rodman, Lewis, M.D.
Rorer, Albert.
Ross, John.
Roux, Julien.
Rugan, Charles.

Rulon, John W.
Rumsey, John.
Rush, John.
Rutter, L. E. H.

Salomon, D
Samuel, David.
Schaeffer, W. L.
Schott, James.
Scott, Charles L
Sharp, John.
Sharpe, J. L.
Sharpless, Brothers.
Sherrerd, Henry D.
Shoemaker, Benjamin H.
Shoemaker, Robert.
Shuff & Wernwag.
Slade, Alfred.
Sleeper, N.
Smiley, T. T.
Smith, Aubrey H., Esq.
Smith, Beaton.
Smith, Charles S.
Smith, Daniel, Jr.
Smith, Edward O.
Smith, Francis Gurney, Esq.
Smith, George K.
Smith, Harrison.
Smith, James B.
Smith, James S., Esq.
Smith, Joseph P.
Smith, J. Fraley.
Smith, Jacob R.
Smith, Richard S.
Smith, Thomas D., Esq.
Smith, Thomas M.
Smith, T.
Smith, William S.
Southworth, D. P.
Steiner, J. P. & Co.
Stevenson & Bowen.
Stewart, W. S.
Stoddart, Curwen.
Stokes, John.
Stotesbury, Thomas P.
Stroud, W. S., M.D.
Strawbridge, George.
Sturgis, Zadock.
Stewart & Brothers.

Suddards, Rev. William.
Sweeney, Thomas W.
Swift, Edwin, Esq.
Syz, John & Co.

Taylor, William Bankson.
Taylor, John D.
Thackara, B.
Thouron, Brothers, Despray.
Thouron, Brothers, Despray, N.Y
Thomas, John.
Thomas, John W.
Thompson, H. C.
Thompson, William D.
Thompson, William R.
Thompson, J. Edgar.
Tomlinson, Joseph.
Townsend, H. C
Townsend, J. B.
Trautwine, J. C.
Traquair, James.
Troth, William P.
Trotter, Joseph H.
Trotter, Edward H.

Vaux, Richard.
Vaux, William S.
Vogdes, John R.
Vogdes, William.

Wagner, Charles M.
Wagner, Tobias.
Wainwright, Jonathan.
Wainwright, William.
Walter, Edwin.
Walker, J. R.
Wannamaker, Charles.
Warnock, William.
Warner, David M.
Warwick, E.
Wattson, Thomas B.
Watson, Charles.
Watson, Thomas, Jr.
Weaver, George J.
Weiner, Heinrich.
Webb, William.
Welsh, Isaac.
Welsh, John.
Welsh, John, Jr.

Welsh, John R.
Welsh, Samuel.
Welsh, W., Jr.
West, Francis, M.D.
West, James.
Wetherill, Dr. William.
Wharton, C. M.
Wharton, Francis A.
Wharton, William, Jr.
Wheeler, John H., Esq.
Whittle, John M.
White, John J.
Wicht & Lankeman.
Wight, Andrew, Jr.
Williams, Charles.
Williams, Charles B.
Williams, Isaac.
Williamson, Passmore.
Williamson, Thomas.
Wilstach, William P.

Wilmer, Cannell & Co.
Wilkins, J. R.
Wilcox, W. T.
Wilson, Stewart.
Wiler, William.
Wilhelm, Frederick.
Winterbottom, H.
Wistar, Mifflin, M.D.
Wolf, Thomas.
Wood, George B.
Wood, Richard D.
Woodward, James S.
Wucherer, J. R.

Yard, Charles W.
Yardley, Samuel.
Yarnall, William.
York, William.

Ziegler, George K.

ERRATA

Wharves, South to Pine, for J. Gerard *Kock*, read *Koch*.

Wharves, Chestnut to Market, for *E.* Beck, read *P.* Beck.

Water street, Market to Arch, for Smith & *Renceway*, read Smith & *Ridgeway*.

Water street, Market to Arch, for *Robinson* & Paul, read *Robeson* & Paul.

Water street, Race to Vine, for D. & V. *Thumm*, read *Thunn*.

www.ingramcontent.com/pod-product-compliance
Lightning Source LLC
Chambersburg PA
CBHW030638030726
47497CB00006B/1847